A New Way of Being at Work

Co-operacy

DALE HUNTER
ANNE BAILEY
BILL TAYLOR

FISHER
BOOKS

*This book is dedicated to the memory of Glenis Rush,
who wanted everything for everybody.*

Publisher: Bill Fisher
                  Helen Fisher
                  Howard W. Fisher

Managing Editor: Sarah Trotta

Original design
and production: Graeme Leather

Production
Manager, U.S.:   Deanie Wood

Cover design: Randy Schultz

First published in New Zealand
in 1997 by Tandem Press

**Library of Congress
Cataloging-in-Publication Data**

Hunter, Dale, 1943–
        Co-operacy : a new way of being at
work / Dale Hunter, Anne Bailey, Bill
Taylor.
                p.   cm.
        Originally published: Auckland :
Tandem Press, 1997.
        Includes bibliographical references
and index.
        ISBN 1-55561-162-1
        1. Teams in the workplace. 2.
Cooperation. 3. Consensus (Social
sciences) 4. Group problem solving.
I. Bailey, Anne, 1944– . II.Taylor, Bill,
1942– . III. Title.
HD66.H856 1998
658.4'02—dc21   98-10414
                                     CIP

Copyright © 1997, 1998 Dale
Hunter, Anne Bailey, Bill Taylor

Printed in the U.S.A.
10 9   8 7 6 5 4 3 2 1

BUDDHA'S ZEN

Buddha said:
I consider the positions of kings and rulers as that of dust motes. I observe treasures of gold and gems as so many bricks and pebbles. I look upon the finest silken robes as tattered rags.

I see myriad worlds of the universe as small seeds of fruit, and the greatest lake in India as a drop of oil on my foot. I perceive the teachings of the world to be the illusion of magicians.

I discern the highest conception of emancipation as a golden brocade in a dream, and view the holy path of the illuminated ones as flowers appearing in one's eyes.

I see meditation as a pillar of a mountain, Nirvana as a nightmare of daytime. I look upon the judgment of right and wrong as the serpentine dance of a dragon, and the rise and fall of beliefs as but traces left by the four seasons.

PAUL REPS AND NYOGEN SENZAKI (COMPILERS). *ZEN FLESH, ZEN BONES.* (BOSTON & LONDON: SHAMBALA, 1994)

Contents

PART THREE – PROCESSES FOR CO-OPERACY

THANK YOU

Thank you David Duignan, our Zenergy co-director and manager, for your partnership and encouragement in having this book happen. And for keeping the business going while Anne and Dale took chunks of time out to write this book.

Thank you John Heron, facilitator and author, for your generosity in critiquing the draft of the book and making many insightful suggestions.

Thank you Len Jeffs for your support and encouragement and long-term commitment to co-operacy over many years of community development work.

Thank you Hamish Brown, Zenergy apprentice, for taking part in many philosophical conversations to clarify the concepts described in the book.

Thank you Bob Ross and Helen Benton for your partnership in publishing our books and the use of your lovely beach cottage as a writing refuge.

Thank you to our editor Graeme Leather for being fun to work with for the third time.

Thank you to our communities, development groups, families and other loved ones for being there.

Arohanui
Dale, Anne and Bill

Introduction

This is a friendly book that we hope will get you thinking. Its purpose is to explore and develop ways in which working together co-operatively as peers can become easier, more effective and more accessible. We encourage you to think about and respond to our ideas. You may agree or disagree. Hopefully, you will respond sufficiently strongly one way or another to talk to others and get some dialog going among your work colleagues and friends. You may also like to have some dialog with us, perhaps through e-mail.

We have already written two books on the same subject—*The Zen of Groups: A Handbook for People Meeting with a Purpose* and *The Art of Facilitation*. Both books focus on working in groups—how to be an effective participant in groups and how to facilitate groups. The content of the three books is part of a growing body of knowledge that we call the "technology of co-operacy."

We believe the world of work and business is at a crossroads. Computer technology has become the major shaper of organizations. The industrial age is reaching an end, and we are at the beginning of a new era referred to by some as the *post-industrial age*. It is clear that the way we think about work and relate to one another will change and is indeed already changing.

Among these large-scale changes is an opportunity for major shifts to occur in the nature of human interaction—in the ways we think about and relate to ourselves and one another. We have an opportunity to consider how we want to be as human beings in the future. We can become more human in the best sense. We can learn to truly value ourselves and each other as perfect equals. Alternatively, we can further objectify ourselves and others into commodities and things, and value them according to their usefulness in economic or status terms.

In a wider context, we can learn to value and protect our environment—our world—and become its guardians, or we can continue to use up irreplaceable natural resources, destroy other forms of life, kill one another, pollute the planet and destroy its ability to sustain life. The choices have never been so clear.

Many people have raised their awareness through personal-development work of many kinds—spiritual, emotional, physical, creative and psychic work associated with the human-potential movement. Some leaders in this area say we are entering a new age of human awareness, indicated through astrology or other mystical experiences. There is also a body of thought that believes we have the ability to create our own reality.

If human development toward an enhanced way of being is even a dim possibility, we want to contribute to it. We want to expand on that possibility to its fullest and richest, and we invite you to be our partners and co-creators in this. This is a path and a journey that enlivens us.

If we think of this new way of being as a hologram, then this book is a piece of it. Many pieces are being developed by many people. And these pieces do not necessarily fit together neatly. That is not important at this stage—the beginning of a new era or paradigm. What is important for us is to make a contribution to a new way of being through our work in developing practical frameworks, methods and processes that can be a resource for others exploring the possibilities of whole-person, co-operative, peer-partnership approach to living and working.

THE STRUCTURE OF THE BOOK

This book is written in three parts. The first part, *Introducing Co-operacy*, contains the key ideas that influence our thinking. Chapter 1 addresses the big picture, the context of this book. Chapter 2 explores the meaning of peer and "peerness." Chapter 3 explores ideas around "whole personhood." Chapters 4, 5, 6 and 7 explore power, alignment, conflict and spirituality. Chapter 8 explores the "shadow side" of peer relationships.

Part Two, *Applying Co-operacy*, explores a variety of relationships within which the peer approach can be applied. These are teams, coaching, mentoring, peer counseling, peer-development groups, peer reflection, peer inquiry and peer organizations. Chapter 17 examines the issues and challenges involved in transforming an organization.

Part Three of the book, *Processes for Co-operacy*, details a variety of exercises you can use to help develop peer partnerships and co-operacy. Use them either as given or modify to suit your specific needs. To make this book complete in itself, we have included some processes from our first two books.

HOW WE WROTE THIS BOOK

This book was written by three people. We worked together and separately. Dale Hunter worked primarily on Parts One and Two. Anne Bailey worked on Part Three. Bill Taylor worked on the overall style, congruence and readability of the book. We all discussed and contributed to each other's work. We laughed, fought and worked through our own issues along the way.

While this is the third book we have written together, we do not consider ourselves experts, either as writers or as co-operators. We are learning from our mistakes, from our failures and from our successes. We wish you an enjoyable and productive read.

We want to challenge your ideas about peer partnerships and co-operacy as you read this book, and ask that you actively participate by taking time to think about the questions we raise under the heading "Thinking Points." There are no right answers to these questions; the value is in the inquiry.

THINKING POINTS

Introducing Co-operacy

PART ONE

Preparing the ground

Life and livelihood ought not to be separated but to flow from the same source, which is spirit, for life and livelihood are about living in depth, living with meaning, purpose, joy and a sense of contributing to the greater community. A spirituality of work is about bringing life and livelihood together again. And Spirit with them.

—MATTHEW FOX

This chapter provides the context and sets the stage for the rest of this book. It offers some of the key big-picture ideas and issues that underpin our thinking. These are: co-operacy, post-industrialism, co-operative organizations, whole personhood, the interaction between personal and work life and community.

CO-OPERACY

Co-operacy is a word we coined to describe the technology of collective or consensus decision-making as distinct from democracy and autocracy. By *technology*, we mean the beliefs, values, methods, processes and techniques that enable collective decision-making to work successfully.

For autocracy to work, there needs to be a widespread belief that, for social organization—including nations, communities, family, workplaces—decisions work best if they are made by one person on behalf of everyone else. For democracy to work, there needs to be a widespread belief that the best decisions for social organization are made by the majority. **For co-operacy to work, there needs to be a widespread belief that the best decisions for social organization are made by involving everyone affected by the decision.**

7

Autocracy is represented historically by the feudal system and currently by dictatorships of various kinds, often military. Democracy is based on majority voting and majority rule. The rise of democracy coincided with the age of industrialization. Co-operacy is represented by co-operative organizations, networks, teams and juries using collective decision-making.

Co-operation is not new, of course. There has always been co-operation among individuals, among organizations, among tribes and among nations. Human life could not have survived without it. Nor is co-operative work new. Beginning with co-operative hunting, gathering, child-rearing, water collection, crop harvest and craft production, co-operative work is part of our heritage.

In this book, we have chosen to take a fresh look at co-operative work, starting from the peer relationship and building from there, rather than exploring the history of co-operatives and co-operative endeavors.

Co-operacy is not yet an integrated system of thought or a coherent philosophy. It may become that in the future, but so far we have only identified some pieces of the puzzle. Other people have other pieces. Because we are standing at the beginning of a new era, the whole picture is not clear yet. A little like the sky on a cloudy day, only some parts of it can be seen—by us, anyway. What we do know is that the old ways of doing things are breaking down or, in some cases, are no longer relevant. New ways, which honor rather than debase humanity, need to be found to replace them.

UNDERPINNING VALUES

Underpinning collective decision-making are beliefs and values, including:

- All people are intrinsically of equal worth.
- Difference is to be valued, honored and celebrated.
- It is possible for all people to live and work together co-operatively.
- The best decisions are made by the people who are affected by them.

Co-operacy
Tree

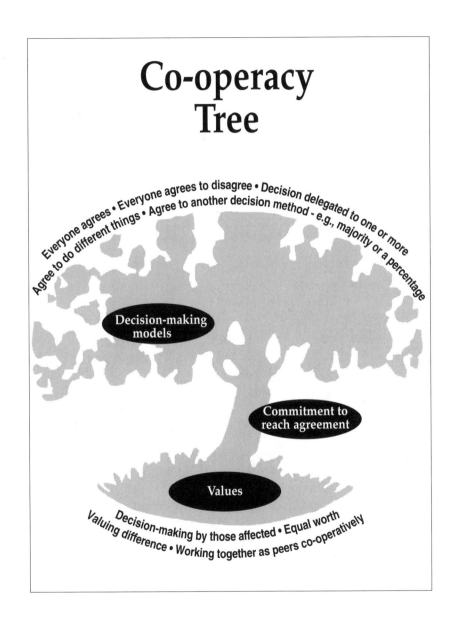

Everyone agrees • Everyone agrees to disagree • Decision delegated to one or more • Agree to do different things • Agree to another decision method - e.g., majority or a percentage

Decision-making models

Commitment to reach agreement

Values

Decision-making by those affected • Equal worth • Valuing difference • Working together as peers co-operatively

For collective decision-making to work, those involved have to have an underlying commitment to reach agreement. This is sometimes spoken of as *an agreement to reach agreement*. This does *not* mean everyone has to agree on everything. Everyone may agree to disagree, delegate the decision-making to one or more people, agree in smaller groups to do different things, or even agree to use a simple majority or another percentage for decision-making as an interim measure.

It *does* mean that everyone is committed to working through issues. Those who disagree have the imperative to propose another course of action and actively take part in the effort to find a solution that will work for everyone. There is no power of unmoving veto. For example: *"This is my position. I'm sticking to it and I won't discuss it."* This is an example of autocracy in reverse.

A co-operative way of working asks a lot of people. It is particularly hard to do because the tools it requires are not part of our normal social "tool kit." We aren't socially conditioned to work co-operatively. As in all forms of decision-making, there are dangers involved. These include the use of veto and the tyranny of peer control. (See chapter 8, *The shadow side.*) We believe, however, that co-operative ways of working need to be developed, invented or rediscovered so they can become a viable choice. We call these new ways of working the "technology of co-operacy."

POST-INDUSTRIALISM

The industrial age was heralded by the industrial revolution and the use of machinery as the primary means of production. This began during the second half of the eighteenth century. The present time is generally referred to as the beginning of the post-industrial age, brought about largely through the explosion of computerized technology and its effects.

Production computerization is both reducing traditional work opportunities and creating a new appreciation of some people's knowledge and creative abilities—the capacities computers cannot yet simulate. Societies are likely to become polarized between these sought-after "knowledge workers" (possibly 20% of all workers) and the vast majority of replaceable, semi-skilled workers who compete for too few jobs.

Post-industrialism is linked to globalization. By this term, we mean the world is perceived as one economic system dominated by multinational organizations. These businesses have the power to move production anywhere in the world where labor and resources are most accessible, and workers are cheaper and more compliant. Already 50 of the 100 largest economies in the world are corporations, not nations.[1]

Globalization drives down wages worldwide, particularly in developed Western countries. Work is transferred offshore to save money. Knowledge workers are less affected by this trend, however. They can be based anywhere in the world. They can keep in touch with their employers by electronic means. Globalization also provides the opportunity for small businesses to operate on a global scale.

How do we want the post-industrial age to be remembered? As a time of polarization, dislocation and alienation on a world-wide scale? Hopefully not! Other possibilities are available.

The possibility we like is that of a co-operative world in which technology serves the greater good of all and supports the transformation of human consciousness. Out of this could come a major shift in human consciousness towards living co-operatively, as one diverse global community in a compassionate and environmentally sustainable society.

A name we like for this is the "Relationship Age" or "Oneness" suggested by Terry Mollner.[2] He sees capitalism and communism as part of the "Material Age," which assumed the universe was an immense number of separate, self-interested parts competing against each other for limited resources. The "Relationship Age" assumes the universe is an immense number of *connected* parts, each of which co-operates with all the others.

CO-OPERATIVE ORGANIZATIONS

We need to make a distinction between co-operative organizations (peer partnerships) and hierarchical organizations. *Peer partnerships* are created among people who see each other as equals and worthy of respect. There may be a great diversity of skills and talents among the individuals but these are not interpreted as making one person better than another or enabling one person to have authority over another without agreement and a clear contract.

Hierarchical organizations are epitomized by the military model, in which decisions are made by a few experienced leaders who have an overview of the situation and responsibility for the movement of large numbers of troops. Commands are passed down quickly from top to bottom, to people who will obey without question. Hierarchies are based on the need to control and command. In civil emergencies, hierarchical organizations may be the best option.

Hierarchical organizations are based on a system of unequal worth. The manager controls the work of the "subordinate" and may be accountable for the work being kept to a certain standard. The manager is presumed to have more skills and experience, is paid more, and can hire and fire. There is an implied hierarchy of worth as well as position. There is a difference in status between managers and workers. Remnants of the officer-soldier class system are still present!

Computer technology has led to an information revolution. Information has become readily and instantly available to many people. In turn it has become less desirable and cost-effective to keep decision-making at the top. The speed of production and change required to meet market demands requires quick decisions. It takes time to get another, more senior person, to make a decision. This person may not have more information anyway, and further, is likely to be so far removed from the situation in question that he or she isn't much help. Time is often a precious resource and in some situations may be more important than a second opinion. For these reasons, the usefulness of hierarchical organizations in business situations is being seriously challenged at present.

Co-operative organizations are a viable alternative to hierarchical organizations in many situations. These organizations include workplaces where there is a diverse range of knowledge and of the skills needed for problem-solving and creative strategizing, and where people expect decision-making involvement. They include: small, specialized organizations, large organizations with discrete business units, and decentralized organizations with bases in far-flung parts of the world that need to respond to local conditions.

THE WHOLE PERSON

A major limitation of hierarchical organizations and industrialization generally has been a tendency to see people within the hierarchy as *things*—units of labor and production. Such objectification has extended to organizations, which have been treated as things to be bought and traded by their owners and shareholders, rather than as communities of people engaged in a productive, collective activity.[3]

Every human being is much more than a unit of labor. We are individuals with many capacities—physical, intellectual, emotional, spiritual, creative, intuitive. Recognition of our wholeness and the need to express ourselves fully is a key to successful interaction among people and within organizations.

We use the expression "whole people in whole organizations" to express this approach. The question arises: What kinds of relationships and organizations will support and nourish the whole person? Our approach is to coin and use the term "peerness"—including peer relationships, peer partnerships and peer organizations—as a distinction that expresses the integration of the whole person and recognizes the concept of whole "personhood" in all human interactions.

The rapid development of human consciousness is making these ideas more acceptable and recognizable. Perhaps more strongly than ever before, many people are aware of their wholeness, their magnificence as beings, and want to live and work in new ways that honor this awareness.

CONNECTING PERSONAL AND WORK LIFE

Industrial production led to the separation of family life from work life. Work was done in the factory and home life was something completely separate. In contrast, many people today can now work from home, whether they are part of a large organization, a small business or are contract workers. New technology makes this an attractive, viable option for many. The difference between work and the rest of life is becoming blurred again.

There is now also much more variety in family configurations—with one-parent families, two-parent families, reconstituted families, gay families, extended families. Child-rearing practices are also changing as a result. Often both parents work full- or part-time and share child-rearing.

In addition, many people (who have the money to pay for it) have taken advantage of opportunities for personal-development training outside traditional state-sponsored educational systems. They find a smorgasbord of opportunities. Some examples are assertiveness training, women's and men's support groups, psychodrama, yoga, martial arts, relationship training, co-counseling, improvisational theater, even journal-writing workshops.

Much of this training aims to increase a sense of personal worth and autonomy—the sense of being in charge or seeking to be in charge of your own life. The desire for autonomy has naturally been reflected in the workplace by raised expectations of involvement in decision-making and meaningful work.

Training opportunities have also increased at many workplaces; for example: adjusting to change, goal- and objective-setting, time management, teamwork training, running effective meetings and facilitation-skills training. All these kinds of classes have a spillover effect on personal endeavors. Skills of setting work goals and objectives are directly transferable to personal and family life. Participants at our effective meeting- and facilitation-training programs often remark on the program's relevance to family life.

COMMUNITY

Humans need to belong—to a family, a tribe, *a community*. Co-operation is the basis of authentic community—a communion of whole people. As work patterns change, other ways of belonging will have to develop to replace the important social aspects of the traditional workplace (the feature new home-based workers miss most). These communities may be physical and local, based around the home. They may be interest-based and operate through clubs and wider networks. They may be virtual communities working through the Internet on a global scale.

One difficulty in introducing whole-person thinking and action into the workplace is the strong social resistance represented by separatist, competitive, hierarchical thinking, which rejects what threatens its very existence. To counter this resistance, we need to establish a support net to hold the new ways of being in place. Otherwise, when an individual tries to introduce changes, the older, stronger paradigm reasserts itself forcefully. To bring about change, individuals need an accompanying technology that includes teamwork and outside support.

Some management thinkers, such as Charles Handy, are addressing the very nature of business and the need to see business organizations as communities of people. Whole people need whole communities that support their new sense of being. Community-building is particularly important for the development of a new paradigm because it becomes the net that holds the paradigm in place and keeps it from lapsing into the old ways. Many groups of people are working to create authentic community —that is, deeply satisfying relationships based on love, tolerance and common values.

CONCLUSION

We have reviewed the major, big-picture trends and ideas that underpin the rest of this book. Big changes happening in the world right now can be seen as positive, negative, a challenge, an opportunity or all of these. We are looking for positive opportunities in the times to come that will enhance human growth and consciousness. We explore these opportunities further in the chapters that follow.

1. "Midwifing: The new consciousness toward the creation of just and sustainable societies." *Lapis* magazine, New York, Issue 3. 1996.
2. Mollner, Terry. "The question of employee ownership" in Michael Ray & Alan Rinzler (editors for the World Business Academy). *The New Paradigm in Business*. Tarcher/Putnam, New York. 1993.
3. Handy, Charles. *The Empty Raincoat*. Hutchinson, London. 1994.

Peer relationships

I may not be attractive, I may not be intelligent, I may not say the right words or do the right things, but I know that the love of myself will open the hearts of all.

—BILLY MILLS

In this chapter we explore what we mean by "peer" and "peer relationships" and how this understanding involves a shift from competitive, exclusive thinking to co-operative, inclusive thinking.

WHAT IS A PEER?

The first question is: What do we mean by "peer"? Do we mean people like us? People with whom we have values, interests, skills and experience in common—those we see as our equals? Are we talking about building relationships and partnerships with those with whom we already have affinity?

It is interesting to consider whom we see as our peers. Is it the people with whom we work? Or is it the people with whom we work, but who also have a similar level of skill and experience? Or is it only the people with whom we work who have similar skills and experience, whom we respect and like? Do age, sex, ethnic grouping, religious beliefs, social class or other factors influence our willingness to recognize others as our peers? How large or small is your peer group—tens, hundreds, thousands, millions? Does your peer group have a hierarchical place above and below other groupings? Is it better or worse than others?

This isn't our way of defining what being a peer is ("peership"). We do not like an exclusive approach that suggests you must meet some conscious or unconscious criteria to become someone's peer. Our approach is inclusive. By *peer*, we mean all those who are of "equal worth" in the fullest spiritual sense. And to us, that means everyone—everyone we can allow to be of equal worth to ourselves. Peership in this sense is not limited, nor is it bestowed. It is a way of being with other people, and a way of being in the world. It is a recognition of the intrinsic worth of every human being on the earth. It is "us" without the luxury of "them."

But isn't this foolish? Aren't some people incompetent, lazy, stupid and bad? Possibly! Then these people are not yet your peers. Peership is a process of allowing others into our hearts and seeing the possibility of their fullest, best selves. Peership is a movable feast; it can be as big as we can accommodate in our hearts.

It is enormously challenging to relate to others in this way—especially in the workplace. It means we have to learn new ways to behave and learn to let go of behaviors that do not support this way of being. It means examining all our patterns of thinking and behaving and being willing to learn and invent a whole new way of being in the world. It means creating a new way of co-operative living.

In different situations, begin to notice how large or small your peer group is. When does your peer group increase? When does it decrease? How does your emotional state affect this?

THINKING POINTS

WHY TAKE THIS CHALLENGE?

We are not saying everybody should or must be peers as we define it. Other kinds of relationships are a completely viable option. We do, however, want to expand on peer relationships as a choice anyone might embrace. First it has to be made clear that peer relationships are a possibility and a free choice.

Taking this challenge is a choice. It is an opportunity to be part of creating a more co-operative world. It's that simple, really. Do you want to be part of this? There are lots of arguments as to why a co-operative world is a good thing. And there are some arguments against it. It is absolutely necessary for the challenge of peership to be a freely made choice, without pressure or blame. We can each validly accept a small group of people as our peers, a large group of people as our peers, or everyone: The same challenge applies. And the challenge is not only with our relationship with others—even more, it is a re-evaluation of our relationship with ourselves.

THINKING POINTS	Discuss or think about the advantages of a more co-operative world. What are the disadvantages? Can co-operation and competition exist side by side? If yes, what would this look like?

RELATING TO OURSELVES

How do we relate to ourselves in a peer environment? This is an interesting question, and it brings up all the thought patterns that get in the way of seeing ourselves and others as equals. Mostly we define ourselves in relation to our differences to others. Compared to another person, we are taller, shorter, fatter, thinner, faster, slower, more or less beautiful, more or less experienced, kinder, more or less emotional, and so on. We notice these differences. In a peer environment, we will honor and celebrate them as part of the rich diversity of humanity.

The problem comes when we imply these differences mean we are better or worse than others. We may also judge ourselves by a standard of some kind—a standard of the average or, more often, a superior standard or ideal that we would like to meet. When we assess ourselves in relation to these standards we often find ourselves wanting.

Yes, I, Dale, am taller, fatter, slower, less intelligent, less beautiful, less sexy and older than my ideal of a woman. I am "deficient" in many ways according to my ideal and can easily get into self-doubt, self-recrimination and just plain depression about my deficiencies. Or I can spend a lot of time trying to get thinner, sexier and more beautiful.

The advertised images we see on TV and other media are all about encouraging us to buy into this kind of thinking and to spend our money on "improving" ourselves.

The thing is, when I see myself as deficient and unworthy, what chance do I have to relate to others as whole, divine, spiritual beings? None at all! I must start with myself. How do I relate to myself? Am I a whole being to be delighted in, loved and appreciated for who I am, with all my idiosyncrasies? (This becomes very confrontational, doesn't it?)

If I keep judging myself in relation to others, I am relating to myself as an object or a thing, rather than as a person—some *thing* to be continually judged as better or worse. And I am doing the same to others. I am thinking in a **competitive-exclusive** way rather than in a **co-operative-inclusive** way. The interesting thing is, both ways are real—as real as thinking can be. It is just a choice as to *which way* we think.

In fact, making this choice is difficult because so much of the everyday world supports the competitive-exclusive way of thinking. We are all defining ourselves and one another in this way. As we grew up we were judged against our siblings and other children. We competed for the attention of our parents, brothers and sisters, teachers and friends. As adults we compete for prizes, scholarships, jobs, sexual partners—all resources that we believe are limited. We also experienced failing, being excluded, left out and shamed as an inevitable part of growing up. We may also have experienced being singled out for praise, rewarded for winning, treated as being special.

We define our own relationship to ourselves in the light of these experiences. We give them meaning and believe we are actually lacking or unworthy—often measured in financial, status or popularity terms—or that we are better or more worthy (measured in the same way).

We give ourselves a whole "negative" or "positive" story, believe it and then act in a way that reinforces this story in the world. In fact we all do this, every one of us—regardless of our capacities and accomplishments.

How we relate to ourselves is the key issue in creating peership. We must make the choice to celebrate ourselves as whole beings with our own unique capacities, strengths and idiosyncrasies. A strong sense of self-esteem is essential if we are to begin the peership journey, which can only start with ourselves. Whenever we continue to relate to ourselves and others as better or worse we have gotten off-track.

We must make this simple but profound shift to develop peership. Until it becomes the prevailing way of thinking the shift must be made individually. It is a free choice. It is more than likely to take a lot of personal-development work to reach this point as an individual. Then it takes a lifetime to train ourselves to retain the new way. Much work is required to catch ourselves when we slip back into the old way over and over again! We, the authors, are still learning to do this and have lots more work to do.

THINKING POINTS

How do you think about yourself in relation to others? Observe your thoughts. Repeat this throughout the day. Which style of thinking describes you at the moment, competitive-exclusive or co-operative-inclusive? —And now? —And now?

Try not to judge yourself—thinking competitively-exclusively is still part of being whole and divine.

RELATING TO OTHERS

We all have the tendency to see others as things, as objects that may or may not please us or be useful to us—"I/it" rather than "I/thou." We learn this approach from others. It is reinforced at work and in many of our relationships. We may rarely have experienced anything other than this way of relating. We even love one another like this: You become an object of my loving; I become an object of yours. This is a relationship that is more likely to lead to manipulation than real connection.

In many cultures, men have historically treated their wives as objects to be owned as property, bosses have treated workers as their property, and parents have treated children this way.

PEER DISTINCTIONS

We find a number of distinctions underlying our definition of peer relationships. They may not be complete but they are the ones we have identified. See if you agree with them.

AUTONOMY

The first step toward relating to others as peers is to have a clear sense of ourselves as separate and autonomous beings, able to think, act and learn for ourselves. The development of autonomy is a process—we develop identity and personality as we mature. The more autonomous we are, the better able we are to co-operate with others. Co-operation *without* autonomy leads to dependence and/or rebellion.

WHOLE PERSON TO WHOLE PERSON

Peer relationships require a whole-person-to-whole-person relationship, an awareness of self and others as full human beings (warts and all), as beings who are divine equals. We are connected through our common divinity. Together we are part of the larger whole. We are all whole beings with different capacities and experiences. Together we create the rich diversity of humanity. (See also "Aspects of whole personhood" in chapter 3.)

CELEBRATING DIFFERENCES

We all have very different personalities, capacities and ways of seeing the world. These differences can be frustrating and annoying at times. However, to the extent we can celebrate these differences, life is richer for everyone. The inability to accept and value cultural and religious differences has led to many of the world's most horrible wars. We all need to work on this aspect as an everyday discipline. It is good practice for us to allow others to be different.

RECOGNITION OF EQUAL WORTH
Peer relationships require recognition of equal worth. No matter how different our circumstances, skills, our educational, social or financial experiences, we are of intrinsic equal worth as human beings.

POWER OF LISTENING
A peer relationship also requires listening, really listening—from the heart and the gut. It involves understanding another's "world" and validating their perceptions without invalidating your own—and it is not always easy to do. (See Process 6, *Mining the gold*, page 166.)

AUTHENTIC SHARING
Relationships are built by sharing of ourselves and recognizing connections. We share who we are, what is important to us, what delights

The Chinese Symbol for Listening

Ear

Eyes

Undivided attention

Heart

us. We share our vulnerability, what hurts us, what has wounded us. We connect. We allow ourselves to be seen and in the process see ourselves as well. Intimacy can be defined as *in-to-me-see*. Intimacy is the basis on which trust and peership can develop. One person sharing his vulnerability and the other person not sharing hers creates an imbalance of power, and the possibility of manipulation and abuse (See chapter 4, *Power,* and Processes 23, *Sharing withholds,* and 32, *Speaking from the heart,* pages 190 and 208).

CONTRACTING

Peership involves negotiating and contracting, starting with a clear statement of preference by each person. These preferences need to be heard.

> *"Yes, I hear that is important to you. It isn't a big deal to me personally, but I want to build our relationship so I will do this particular action."* or *"Yes, I understand and appreciate your feelings. I didn't realize you felt that way. I don't feel comfortable doing X but I could do Y. Would that help?"*

This kind of negotiation is the basis for building a relationship of equality. (See Process 7, *Negotiating and contracting with peers,* page 168.)

ALLOWING SPACE FOR ONE ANOTHER

A peer relationship is dynamic and organic. It grows, changes, develops, keeps moving to new dimensions. We see new aspects of others as we learn more about ourselves. We "discover" the relationship as we go; part of it always remains unseen, mysterious. We need to provide space for one another to change and grow—space for the mysterious to be revealed. If we perceive one another in a fixed way, we may not notice when the other person has changed. Also, if we relate to people based on past experience, we will tend to hold them back and keep them stuck. Giving someone "space" can mean a physical "time out" to be on your own, or it may mean emotional or psychological space. (See also "Autonomy and co-operation," page 47.) Some people need a lot more space than others. Are you willing to claim your own space and provide it for others?

GROWING EMOTIONAL COMPETENCE

An important part of the journey towards true peer relationships is the development of emotional competence; that is, the ability to recognize and process our own distress and patterned behavior. We sometimes call this distress *baggage*—it *is* like taking your emotional suitcases with you everywhere and tripping over them. We all do this, of course, but baggage makes it difficult to connect with others. We all spend a lot of our time acting in patterned ways—acting from past unhealed distress. Patterned behavior is something to be aware of in ourselves and to be tolerant of in others. Peer-counseling techniques are a useful way of healing some past hurts and freeing ourselves to be more spontaneous. (See chapter 12, *Peer counseling.*)

Clearing and completion processes also help keep us from collecting additional distress. (See Processes 24 to 27, pages 193-199.) Freed of distress, we are connected to our whole selves; we are able to be in touch with our love for others. At any moment we are either connected or we are not—difficult, isn't it? But don't expect to be distress-free all the time. Distress cannot be thrown away like a piece of trash. Distress needs to be healed, and healing can take a while sometimes—even a long time. Be content with any progress you make, however small.

ACKNOWLEDGMENT

Affirmation and acknowledgment of ourselves and others is essential if we want to create true peer relationships. When we acknowledge others we *both* expand—we become more whole, more empowered. We need acknowledgment, from ourselves *and* others, as much as we need food! We can starve without it. It is the element most missing in many organizations, including co-operative organizations. Acknowledgment needs to be honest, clean (no "buts") and non-manipulative (not done in order to be liked or to get something). Our "falsity barometers" are very sensitive, so faking acknowledgment never works.

COMMITMENT

From our discussion in this chapter it is clear that creating and maintaining peer relationships is not going to be easy. They require commitment, hard work and ongoing work. The process is never over. It is a journey, a learning curve, an exploration without a final destination. This is the bad news. You may want to consider whether you think the trouble involved is worth it to you. Compare this to other goals to which you have dedicated yourself in the past. Is there something important enough to you that you will persevere no matter how tough the going gets? Is it your children, the investment you have put into your business, the house you have bought?

What is at stake for you in wanting to create a peer relationship? It helps to identify something that will make it worth the hard work of creating and recreating peership. For some people, what is at stake is a belief that ongoing, loving connection is possible.

Consider a relationship that is difficult for you. Reflect on the differences between you and the other person. Now reflect on the connections you have with that person. Where do you put most of your energy in this relationship?

THINKING POINTS

CHAPTER 3

Whole personhood

Drinking tea, desires diminish and I come to see the ancient secret of happiness: wanting what I already have, inhabiting the life that is already mine.

—THE MINISTER OF LEAVES, FROM A WONDERFUL CANISTER OF CALIFORNIA CARDAMOM-CINNAMON WARM THE HEART TEA BY THE REPUBLIC OF TEA

We have already introduced the idea of *whole personhood*—someone who can fully express his or her many aspects and capacities—and also the notion of relating to others as whole beings. In this chapter we explore the concept further.

HUMAN CAPACITIES

We believe our human capacities, known and unknown, conscious and unconscious, interweave and merge into one another to create a whole.

With the rise of science, the dominant Western culture has given prominence to the rational, conceptual, thinking aspects of our humanness at the expense of our other capacities. We have suppressed these other capacities, particularly the non-rational ones, treating them as less important and some even as dangerous; for example, psychic abilities. Individually and collectively, we have become unbalanced as a result. We have lost access to our wholeness.

Scientific reductionism is now under assault from within, particularly in the area of quantum physics. To put the whole-person approach in a theoretical framework, quantum theorist David Bohm says: "Quantum theory implies that the universe is basically an indivisible whole even though on a larger scale it may be represented approximately as divisible into separately existing parts." (As quoted in *The Fifth Discipline* by Peter Senge.)

Today, many people recognize that this kind of imbalance has contributed to the world environmental crisis. Further, many people see that capacities which cannot be readily duplicated by technology—intuitive, creative and psychic—are needed to solve our global problems. As individuals, we are out of balance in the same way the world environment is out of balance. One cannot be separated from the other.

To address our internal imbalance it is useful to explore the various human capacities we can identify and get a sense of their diversity. Then, by developing our various capacities, we can rebalance our beings individually in more harmonious ways.

A model of whole personhood that you may find helpful appears on page 28. When you consider this model, keep in mind it is just that—a model. It is not the truth; it is one *representation* of the truth. In the process of dividing our wholeness into compartments, something is lost; we cannot replicate complex truth exactly.

You may want to design your own model of whole personhood. What aspects of the "whole you" do you see? Try the same exercise in a group. What categories do people invent? Are they similar, or different? Can the group agree on one model?

THINKING POINTS

ASPECTS OF WHOLE PERSONHOOD

CONCEPTUAL: The ability to think in a rational way, creating ideas and concepts. We categorize and divide things. We create patterns. We understand.

Aspects of whole personhood

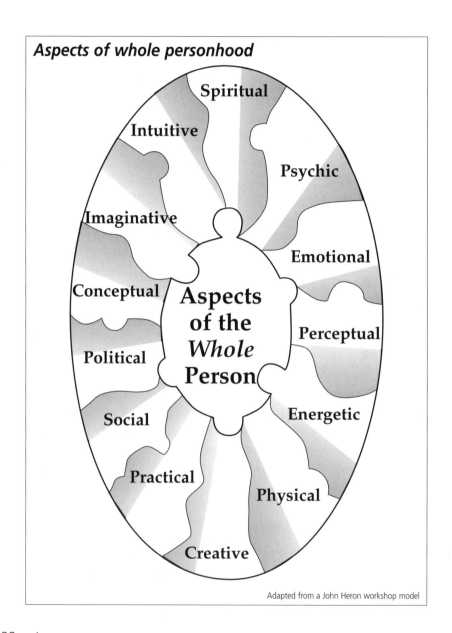

Spiritual

Intuitive

Psychic

Imaginative

Emotional

Conceptual

Aspects of the *Whole* Person

Perceptual

Political

Social

Energetic

Practical

Physical

Creative

Adapted from a John Heron workshop model

SOCIAL: The capacity to enjoy the presence of others and contribute to their enjoyment.

POLITICAL: The ability to act with others to bring about change.

IMAGINATIVE: The ability to put images and ideas together in ways not already thought of.

INTUITIVE: The ability to know things through non-rational processes.

SPIRITUAL: The capacity to connect with the divine and sacred.

PSYCHIC: The many abilities that enable access to the more subtle realms.

EMOTIONAL: The capacity to experience love, fear, grief and anger and their subtle distinctions.

PERCEPTUAL: The ability to absorb information through the five bodily senses used for sight, sound, touch, smell and taste.

ENERGETIC: The capacity to sense energy and use this ability to enhance our knowledge about ourselves and others.

PHYSICAL: The capacity to experience, be in tune with and act with our bodies.

PRACTICAL: The ability to do things—to carry out purposeful action.

CREATIVE: The ability to bring new forms into being.

DIMENSIONS OF WHOLE BEING

The model on page 28 describes some aspects of whole being we can distinguish on a personal level. But this is not the only level. Wholeness is present at all levels and in all domains. Wholeness can be present in relationships, organizations and community. Wholeness in a world context includes the Earth as a whole, as an organism that is alive and intelligent (the Gaia hypothesis). In this whole, human beings are one part. In the cosmos, the whole is everything we can think of, sense or imagine. Earth and the galaxy including the Earth are a part of this. Similarly, in the subtle/psychic domains there exists the whole and its parts—for example, all ancestors and my grandma. There are internal, interpersonal, cultural, ecological and transplanetary wholes and parts.

THE PARADOX OF BEING WHOLE

How do we get to be whole as an experience rather than as a thought? In the everyday world of thinking and doing, this is difficult. The thinking/doing world is the world of discrimination, polarities and separation. The "doing world" is accessed through thinking. Thoughts come and go, and things occur in parts rather than in "wholes." We create wholes by holding the parts together in our attention. When we break our attention, the whole falls back into parts. We appear incomplete to ourselves because of the difficulty of holding all parts in our thoughts at the same time. We appear to ourselves as separate, alone, better/worse and different. Other people appear the same way. In this world we often feel dissatisfied and think something is missing. We can tell we have access to some of it but not all of it. We can think about wholes, but cannot access them necessarily.

This is where the "being world" comes in handy. The being world accesses through *perceiving the whole,* not thinking. We call that *presencing.* To access parts in the being world it is necessary to distinguish among them by focusing attention on one at a time. When we stop focusing on a particular element, it falls back into the whole. We occur to ourselves as whole and complete. Others occur to themselves the same way. We have access to others through presencing that connection.

Dissatisfaction has no place in the being world, because that world is whole and complete *as it is.* Dissatisfaction exists in the doing world because we cannot be whole in that context except for short periods. We gain access to our wholeness through the being world.

ENTRY INTO THE DOMAIN OF BEING

How do you access the domain of being? It's one thing to talk about it, but how do you get there? *Getting to being involves going beyond thinking.* You could say it means getting to a place where thinking gets tired of itself, and we start to notice the spaces between thoughts.

There are many doorways to being. We can start by thinking of ourselves as whole. We can think about the possibility of being whole and that all our capacities are present in conscious or unconscious forms. We are "all here." Nothing is missing. We can develop a belief system about it so we know, in our thinking, that it is possible to be this way.

Then we can develop some practices to help us reach the state of being. Some practices, such as meditation, yoga and tai chi were designed specifically for this purpose. Other processes include Avatar, the Forum, co-counseling and rebirthing. Playing or listening to music and practicing or appreciating other art forms can provide access. Being in nature, running or swimming are also a way in. And any practice that transcends thought works, too. You may also enter simply by being receptive to the ever-present feeling of being. It's a little like riding a bicycle. It's easy when you know how, but it is hard to begin—until you get your balance.

We use the experience of community building as a way of accessing being—working with a group of people and using the M. Scott Peck model. (See chapter 13.) The four stages involved—pseudo-community, chaos and conflict, emptiness, and authentic community—take the group beyond thinking and into emptiness as part of the group process. You can use the power of group synergy to get there with velocity. When thinking tires and spaces exist, presence can arise in the spaces.

Presence is the material or fabric of being. Presence is experienced as "nothing" or "being mindful." There is nothing missing in being. It is the whole, not the part. In the space of wholeness, that is all there is. Experiencing wholeness in a group is potent because the whole being of the group is also readily available.

BEING AND DOING

What is the usefulness of the two worlds of being and doing? And are there other worlds, too? It seems likely.

There is nothing wrong with the doing world. This world has allowed the intellect to develop, with all the creations that have come from that, including science and philosophy. The doing world is the world of discrimination.

The downside is that this is also the world of separation and suffering. To ground ourselves totally in this world is dissatisfying and limits our access to the being world.

The being world is the world of wholes. There is no need to do anything in the being world. In this world it is fine to do nothing. In this world there is no suffering because suffering is not identified with pain, grief, hunger or thirst. Suffering comes from perceiving ourselves as separate and alone. In the being world, action is a conscious choice—to be in action.

The downside of the being world can be inaction. To ground ourselves *primarily* (not totally) in the being world is, however, eminently satisfying, and access to the doing world is easy—through what we call "being-in-action."

STAYING IN BEING

Getting access to the being state is one thing. What about staying there? Usually we slip out again almost immediately—back into the doing world.

Again, the analogy of learning to ride a bicycle helps describe this effort. We need to keep going back into the doing world until we learn to access the being world at will. Then we have achieved balance—we can experience being and being-in-action at will.

People sometimes tell us they find it difficult to apply their new learning/knowing because they are in a work environment where the others are "not whole people." What they are really saying is their work environment makes it difficult for them to access *their own* wholeness. It's not really about others, it is about themselves.

What provides access to wholeness? The state of being or beingness allows wholeness to appear or enables us to experience our wholeness. When anyone appears "not whole" to you, the only place to look for change is to yourself.

A person experiencing being him- or herself recognizes everyone else as whole. The paradox is that *the only access we ever have to this is through recognizing or standing up for our own wholeness.*

When we perceive other people as lacking it indicates that in some way we are not seeing ourselves as whole. Fixing each other isn't the answer ("If only my friend were more whole!"). We can only "fix" ourselves. For example, I may not like seeing old people or fat people, but that is probably because I fear getting old or fat.

How can people be anything other than our peers when we reach out from a position of our own wholeness? From that position, there are only peers and more peers and more peers.

Sometimes people mistake feeling "good" or expansive or in love with the world as the whole of the being state. This is not the essence of being, though it is part of it. Being is a state, not an emotion. You can feel happy, sad, or any number of different emotions while in the being state. You will, however, notice a sense of wholeness—expressed sometimes as "emptiness" or "fullness" when in this state.

BEING-IN-ACTION IS AN ACT OF CREATION

In the domain of being, we may *choose* to be in action. The state of being-in-action is an act of creation or, if it involves another, co-creation. We can be creative in all our activities, whether they be thinking, problem-solving or making things. We know of no limits to the creativity of humanity.

Humans are naturally creative. We are creative at play as children: We make things up, we fantasize, we use our imaginations and act them out in play. As we grow into adulthood we often tell ourselves or are told by others that we are not artistic or creative, and then we begin to restrict ourselves from using our creative "muscles." We shut down an important part of ourselves and deny ourselves the opportunity to be fully ourselves.

Creativity flourishes in an atmosphere of acceptance, lightness and stimulation of our senses and minds. To the extent we allow creativity to emerge, it grows and develops. We become creatively "self-expressed," creatively competent. Creativity is one human capacity that computer technology is unable to replicate so far. Unfortunately, we can become creatively incompetent through atrophy of our creative capacity.

We also need to watch out for the doing-domain definition of creativity, which is oriented to looking at everything as parts. Western compartmentalization of life says that some activities are creative and some are not—painting a picture is creative, but painting a house is not; ballet is creative, but soccer is not. We unnecessarily restrict ourselves in this way. In many indigenous cultures there is no word for the "arts"—they are so much a part of everyday life there is no need for such a concept. For these cultures, singing, cooking, dancing, gathering food, making clothes, mats and containers are integral to being-in-action in everyday life.

Creative thinking usually involves certain steps. An idea is followed by divergent and lateral thinking, which in turn is followed by an incubation period as things get shuffled around in the unconscious. Then a new idea, perhaps related to or an amalgam of the old, emerges.

Creative thinking has been popularized in recent years by people like Edward De Bono, who encourages us to use lateral thinking and other techniques to tap into our creativity.

CONCLUSION

The paradox of whole personhood is that, no matter what we see as missing or deficient in ourselves, we are actually whole anyway. Nor is it a matter of when we are most whole—as a baby, youth, adult or old person. We are *always* whole. We must always remind ourselves of this.

THINKING POINTS	Start to notice your own areas of creativity and your own creative processes at work. When are you creative?

Power

*The dangerous logic of power has forced
all of human society toward ever-greater
systems of domination, even as our world so
obviously suffers from the unending abuses
such competition-driven systems create.*

—MICHAEL SKY

Power in itself is a neutral force. It exists. It can be used or misused. Power, however, is always a factor to be addressed in peer relationships because relationships usually involve power differences. Power differences are just that—difference. They do not need to be changed but they do need to be acknowledged. If they remain unacknowledged they can lead to oppressive behaviors easily.

In addition, some social norms oppressively reinforce our behavior. Power differences in areas such as gender, age, ethnicity, sexual preference, intelligence and disability are reflected in stereotyped behavior. They are also built into the structure and legal fabric of societies.

Power differences are also the basis of most professional relationships involving an expert and a client. Well-trained professionals learn to work ethically and not to abuse this power.

This chapter addresses power issues from a number of perspectives: personal, in relationships, groups, organizations and society—and in relation to sex and money.

PERSONAL POWER
Where does personal power come from? What gives someone a sense of

personal power? We have found that integrity is the basis of personal power. What is the basis of integrity? It is the state of being whole, entire or undiminished. It comes from experiencing ourselves as whole, separate yet connected beings. If we feel diminished by others and doubt ourselves, we lose power and begin to disconnect from our essence; we are "out of integrity." Our power supply comes from being connected, from having integrity with ourselves and others.

POWER IN RELATIONSHIPS

All relationships are imbued with power issues. We have been manipulated and controlled all our lives, starting from babyhood. Because this is how we were treated, it is also how we have learned to behave.

Disconnected from our whole selves, we see others as objects and seek to manipulate, control and dominate them. That is what one does with objects; one controls them and moves them around. Or, if we don't try to manipulate others, we allow ourselves to be controlled and dominated by others.

We seek to control or are controlled unconsciously for the most part. Even if we are conscious of being controlled, we may take it for granted. We don't necessarily like it! We feel dissatisfied. We resist. We sabotage. We rebel. Underneath oppressive, abusive and manipulative behaviors are always feelings of powerlessness and hurt. We abuse others because we have been abused.

Power issues arise in all relationships in subtle and unsubtle ways. In peer relationships we need to learn to recognize and work through these issues. Start by becoming aware of your own power patterns.

You may be getting along fine with someone until suddenly you come up against power issues. This often happens as you become more intimate with another person. Perhaps you are not setting clear limits and boundaries for yourself and begin to feel taken over.

The bottom line is always "equal worth as whole beings." That means unlearning behavior not based on this concept. It is not OK to dominate others, whether they are friends, colleagues, children, women, parents, old people or anyone else who is less physically, mentally or emotionally strong than we are. Nor is it OK to be dominated yourself.

When do you seek to have power over others? How do you achieve this? How does it feel? How do you give away your power to others? How does that feel? Do you do this with the same people or different people? Talk to a trusted friend or colleague about what you notice. Are you willing to work on letting go of these behaviors? It isn't easy. Notice others' patterns and try not to buy into them.

THINKING POINTS

The concept of equal worth as whole beings does not, however, mean treating every person as if he or she has equal talent, skills, abilities, capacities and resources. The idea that everyone must be equal in every way is a recipe for disaster. This is just another kind of coercion and domination—the domination of sameness, mediocrity or the lowest common denominator.

What are the different and complementary skills, talents and capacities each person has? Do we give more weight to some rather than others? Why? How can we share power more equitably? We need to work at these issues constantly. This may include getting help from a facilitator or relationship counselor.

Relationships can become stuck if power issues are not addressed. It is easy over time to fall into roles where one person becomes dominant and the other dominated. This is particularly easy if one person has more skills, experience or knowledge than the other.

POWER AND SEX

Power has long been associated with gender and sex. The male has power over the female and has dominated her and treated her as property in many parts of the world with the support of law. The sexual act can be used to assert power. This is what rape is about. Changing this power dynamic is the basis of feminist thinking and work. And lots more work needs to be done.

In traditional marriage, disparity of power was institutionalized, with the husband having legal and moral power over his wife. Dominant/dominated patterns can easily become oppressor/victim patterns, with the oppressor feeling frustrated and the victim, powerless. We may have watched these patterns played out in our own families and now find ourselves playing out the same roles. Do we know how to relate in any other way?

These patterns need to be unlearned or interrupted. That takes effort. It takes going against the flow of how things always have been. Are you prepared to put in the work to change ingrained habits that may go back thousands of years?

POWER AND MONEY

What about the relationship between power and money? There is lots of distress regarding money and all kinds of habitual responses to it in our society. When distress is high, power struggles erupt. Think about your own hopes and then your worst fears where money is concerned. Notice your own and others' patterns. Some people have scarcity patterns and keep themselves on a tight budget. Others may have addictive patterns and spend recklessly. Still others may have hope-for-the-best patterns and not plan much for the future.

Consider the patterns you and your partners have before you create a business together. The patterns in your life and in your business are likely to be the same. A way to uncover them is to talk about them. Some families don't talk about money (or sex or death) in front of the children. If this is your pattern and it's operating in your business, be sure to interrupt it!

Discuss money as an open conversation. What are your expectations as far as earning it, saving it, investing it? Is it OK for some partners to earn more, some less? What are the allaround differences in your attitudes toward money? (For example, do any of these words describe your attitude toward money: relaxed, jealous, competitive, joyful? Or does some other word sum up your feeling?)

Power in business is often related to the distribution of shares or capital investment. A pecking order can develop in which the bigger investors are given more weight in discussions as well as decision-making privileges.

A peer organization often involves different levels of investment. This needs to be discussed openly also. What does this mean in practice for each of you? Ask one another what each of your expectations is regarding money, and record the answers. Get everything out in the open—have clear legal contracts. What decisions will the bigger investors want to be involved in: the larger financial decisions?—capital investment? If money is short, what will the priorities be? Do you have bottom-line and contingency arrangements?

We have made different kinds of monetary arrangements in our organization. We recognized the value of a time investment as well as money when allocating shares. We have at different times all earned different amounts. Sometimes we agree to pool our incomes. There isn't one right answer. Use what works and is congruent with your beliefs.

Arguments around money are often about other issues as well. Uncover these. What beliefs and fears are underneath? All our childhood distress around money and family arguments around this will come up. Share what you are feeling: *"This reminds me of when Dad went to the races and spent the housekeeping money . . ."*

Remember, money is a resource like time, skills, talent and abilities. Are you keeping the money conversation in proportion or letting it oppress you?

> What are your patterns around money? What are your hopes and fears? What were your parents' patterns? Your father's? Your mother's? How are your own patterns similar?

T H I N K I N G
P O I N T S

SOME THOUGHTS ABOUT POWER FROM OTHERS

Excellent material has been written on the subject of power. Here is a taste of some of what is available in libraries and bookstores for you.

John Heron thinks it is most helpful to think of power in terms of three kinds of decision-making:

- deciding for others—hierarchy, power over
- deciding with others—co-operation, power with
- deciding for ourselves—autonomy, power within

In an oppressive society, the first of these is used extensively to suppress the other two. In a liberated society, the first is used only to enhance the other two. Thus Heron believes that a society based on peership and co-operacy "will involve not only autonomy but also, in some situations, an element of appropriate hierarchy, which means a person thinking and deciding for others in order to develop their future autonomy and co-operation." John Heron says:

> *Such situations include parenting, certain types of training and professional practice, and when a peer is asked to take on a hierarchical role for an agreed time and an agreed purpose. So you may want your peer to use an intensive contract as your counselor in co-counseling. A group may appoint someone to make decisions for them in their absence, or to [facilitate] for them in their presence . . .*

> *Unless this element of appropriate hierarchy is clearly made explicit, co-operacy could become a front for the hidden play of inappropriate (that is, controlling and dominating) hierarchy.*

The author Starhawk, in her book *Truth or Dare,* distinguishes among three kinds of power: power over, power from within and power with. "Power over" comes from estrangement and war, "power from within" arises from our sense of connection to and bonding with others and the environment. "Power with" comes from a willingness to listen to and respect one another and take action together.

When we are upset and vulnerable, we tend to be more sensitive to power differences. We may seek to reduce our fear of being controlled by controlling others. In *The Celestine Prophecy* James Redfield explains it as the way we take energy from one another. He describes four main ways we take each other's energy: through intimidation, interrogation, aloofness and a poor-me approach. Each of us has a dominant form of stealing energy.

Michael Sky, in *Sexual Peace: Beyond the Dominator Virus*, says that the world has had a dominator culture—patriarchy—for the past several thousand years. Because evolution favors adapting to the prevailing culture, "human evolution has favored the means and methods of domination. All the ways of a dominator culture have continually evolved and improved, while all the essentials of a partnership culture (unadaptive traits in a patriarchal world) have atrophied."

POWER IN GROUPS

In our book *The Zen of Groups*, we discussed power in groups. This section is based on that work. Here are some different types of power found in groups:

POSITIONAL POWER: One person in the group has a more powerful position than other group members in the organization or community of which the group is a part. This person may be a manager, elected representative, government worker, teacher or other important person. People with positional power usually have more power in the group than the other individuals. They will be listened to more carefully and their opinions given more weight. Positional power is bestowed from outside the group and recognized within the group. Positional power may include the ability to override group decisions by intervening outside the group.

ASSIGNED POWER: When a group assigns a particular role to a group member, that person collects greater power. Such a role could be as a group or project leader, facilitator, teacher, record-keeper, financial controller, spokesperson for the group, coach or team captain. Assigned power is given by the group and withdrawn by the group.

KNOWLEDGE POWER: A group member has a specialist's knowledge or experience in an area related to the work of the group. The person may be a computer expert, accountant, town planner, medical professional, expert in a language or culture, and so on. The knowledge and experience need to be relevant to the group. Often knowledge power is held by group members who already have positional or assigned power.

PERSONAL POWER: A person, through personal skills and qualities, is seen as a guide or leader by group members. The person may have skills in communication or have charisma related to his or her life experience. This person may not have a position of assigned power within the group or any positional power. Other factors that can influence personal power include age, sex, ethnic background, marital status, length of involvement in the group, wealth or physical appearance.

FACTIONAL POWER: Several people within a group act together in an organized way to influence or dominate the group process or decision-making. The degree to which a faction is powerful in a group may depend on the number of people involved, whether they also have positional or other kinds of power, and whether or not they form a majority.

OCCASIONAL POWER: Someone has power for a short period. For example, someone may have particular resources wanted by the group for a particular purpose: Perhaps a group member has access to food and water when the others are hungry and thirsty.

Power is a factor in every group, and it will be useful for you to identify and be aware of how it is expressed. Recurring conflict in a group is often the result of unclear or unrecognized power relationships.

Group members can become skilled at recognizing, clarifying and working through power issues. The power relationships of a group can become conscious or spoken through group exercises. (See Processes 13, *Exploring power*, 14, *Mapping power* and 15, *Power and money*.)

POWER AND ORGANIZATIONS

Power in organizations can be informal, as discussed in chapter 2, or structural; that is, built into the formal structure of the organization.

Power that is related to the structure of an organization is *positional power.* Hierarchical organizations rely heavily on positional power to maintain control. A manager can direct staff members to act and can fire them if they refuse. This kind of power—to hire, fire and direct—affects all the relationships in a hierarchical organization, even if the manager does not exert this power directly. Whether it is used or not, the power is still there. It is not possible to create an equal relationship in this situation.

In peer organizations, all six kinds of power discussed under "Power in groups" will be seen. (See also chapter 16, *Peer organizations.*)

What do you see as the key issues around power? How have you addressed them?	*THINKING POINTS*

Alignment

Out beyond ideas of rightdoing and wrongdoing
There is a field
I will meet you there
When the soul lies down in that grass
The world is too full to talk about

—*RUMI*

This chapter explores the different aspects of alignment. Tremendous energy, often called *synergy,* is available when we come together in groups and organizations. But access to synergy does not happen automatically. Many organizations never get beyond achieving a fraction of their potential. They miss out on the transformational energy available from alignment.

When souls sing together, the universe sings too; ice melts and the oceans part. The power of alignment does not require large numbers to be effective. Two or three people gathered together can create big shifts in the world. Twelve people designed the Constitution of the United States.

To work together co-operatively, groups of diverse people (any two or more) must work together to develop ways to create and maintain alignment. By *alignment,* we mean the bringing together of hearts and minds, and more, in such a way that the energies and efforts of everyone will lead to coordinated and synergistic action. It is a whole-person concept: people coming together with all their talents to take creative action.

The alignment of the "body" of whole people is the aim. The contribution of head or heart alone will not create synergy. If the heads agree but the hearts aren't engaged, synergistic action isn't possible.

Similarly, it won't work if the hearts beat as one but the heads disagree. More than the head and the heart are involved, actually. For alignment to occur, "whole-body" energies, of which the head and the heart are just part, are involved.

Alignment does not seek to override differences. It does require a large enough space to recognize and celebrate these differences. Nor does it mean there is no room for autonomous thinking or that conflict and chaos must be inhibited. For alignment to occur, there must be room for all these elements.

ALIGNMENT AND AGREEMENT

The difference between alignment and agreement is shown in the diagram below. Agreement occurs at the level of mind only, while alignment involves the person in every respect. As you can see, alignment is more powerful than agreement—it calls us to action. However, sometimes agreement is as far as we can get. That is OK, too.

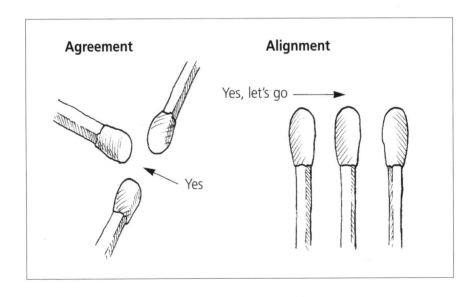

Collective decision-making or consensus is more likely to create alignment than majority decision-making. (See Process 50, *Consensus decision-making*.)

SPACE TO BE DIFFERENT

Each of us has beliefs and opinions on just about everything—gender, age, sexuality, ethnicity, morals, politics, spirituality and so on. We have rational and irrational beliefs. *Peer-relatedness* involves becoming conscious about the beliefs, opinions and judgments that limit our relationships with ourselves and others by dividing us. These "limiting" beliefs are the ones it is important to let go of. Stereotyping and judgments are based on them; for example: *"You are X ethnic group. All Xs do Y. I don't like Y; therefore I don't like you."* The more of this kind of separating, limiting thinking we can let go of, the more connected and loving we can be.

It is important to acknowledge and celebrate differences and bring these fully into our relationships. For example, cultural differences, when they are valued, can add immensely to the richness of a relationship, an organization and a community. We need to develop processes, structures and practices that honor these differences in practical and meaningful ways. Relationships among different genders, ethnic backgrounds and ages need to be handled with sensitivity because they too involve power issues.

In New Zealand, recognition of the relationship between the indigenous Maori people and the European settlers was the basis of the Treaty of Waitangi in 1840. This treaty has become a touchstone on which to begin the challenging task of building a bicultural society in the late twentieth century. The confirmation of the treaty has addressed the practical and spiritual issues involved and begun a healing process for the whole nation. Alignment in this context means *getting bigger*—allowing space for two cultures to be fully recognized and developed, and allowing for people to identify freely with one or both.

By working together on this book and other projects, we have found that allowing more and more space for one another to be authentically different is an important part of our group process. For example: Each of us (Dale, Anne and Bill) brought different skills and knowledge to writing this book. We didn't all try to do the same things or have an equal distribution of effort. We contributed according to our skills; each worked in his or her own preferred way. By valuing one another's contributions, and recognizing the different levels of contribution we made (including financially), we are able to continue working together.

AUTONOMY AND CO-OPERATION

Maintaining the creative tension between autonomy and co-operation in all peer relationships is a key point to bear in mind about alignment. We are spiritual beings connected to one another and all life. We are also our individual capacities and idiosyncrasies—our personality—and these need to be valued and developed in the way we personally see fit, in line with our life purpose. It is fair to say that we can be only as cooperative as we can be autonomous. We need to learn to set boundaries so our autonomy is not compromised. We also need to recognize and respect other people's personal boundaries. This is hard; often we don't recognize someone else's boundaries, or our own, until the line has been crossed.

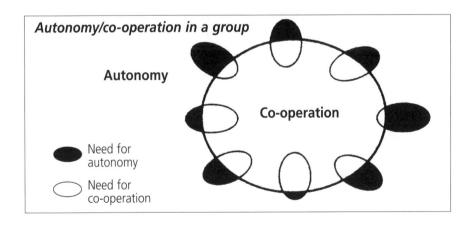

Autonomy/co-operation in a group

Autonomy

Co-operation

● Need for autonomy

○ Need for co-operation

THINKING POINTS

Practice noticing your boundaries. How do you know what they are? What happens when they are crossed? Notice other people's boundaries. How do you know when they have been crossed?

STRUCTURE AND CHAOS

The nature of change and the role of chaos in the change process provides another example of creative tension related to alignment. All theories about the role of chaos, complexity and paradox point to their importance and necessity in the turbulent and complex times in which we live. The same principles apply where the development of a relationship, group or organization is concerned. A developing relationship of any type needs room for chaos as well as structure. A structure that is too strict inhibits change. Creativity will not flourish in an environment of fear and control. It requires a lot of freedom—of the mind and the whole being.

PROCESSES FOR CREATING ALIGNMENT

We offer a range of methods and processes for creating and maintaining alignment. Some are well-known and practiced by most organizations. These include strategic alignment around a purpose, direction, culture, values, principles, plans, goals and policy. They also include management alignment for day-to-day practices, procedures and systems. Mostly these exercises use the power of thinking (the head). If they are carried out well they can also engage the heart.

Engaging the heart is developed through sharing and relationship-building. Organizations often create this unconsciously through such informal processes as sharing experiences ("What happened over the weekend?"), work-organized social outings, helping one another in crises and celebrating successes.

Few organizations seek consciously to develop other kinds of alignment, which are just as important. For example, spiritual alignment can be developed through discovering and internalizing the higher purpose of an organization. Then there is energetic alignment. This is not as well known or practiced but is very important in creating coordinated, harmonious action. Unconsciously every group of people seeks energetic alignment because it feels better to do so and creates a harmonious atmosphere. It can be done by creating rituals and practices that support and enhance your organization's higher purpose.

Alignment on all levels is important. It is a matter of taking all aspects of a person into account (the "whole person") and looking to that person for what is missing or needed in your relationship or organization.

STRATEGIC ALIGNMENT

In a peer working relationship—one in which you are working together with someone else on a project—alignment is required. By this we mean that you agree on a common purpose. You have a written statement, possibly expressed through a vision or mission statement. You will also have more specific goals and/or objectives that set out what you need to realize the vision. These become part of your strategic plan.

In a peer organization you will involve everyone in the planning process so everyone will be committed to and in alignment with the project and one another. It is best to write down your plans. Give everyone copies and review them regularly. Check periodically to see if you are still in alignment. People and circumstances change. Do not assume your group will be in alignment partway through a project just because you started that way. You might plan to have an alignment check once every three months over the course of a year-long project, for example.

When disagreement and conflict arise among those working on the project, it is helpful to return to your vision and goals. Restate them and check to see that everyone involved is still in alignment. You may have lost sight of the big picture. You may be bogged down in detail, or the objectives may need to be rethought to meet the goals better.

You can develop a strategic plan in a number of ways. If possible, use an outside facilitator to walk you through the steps. Discuss the model you will use with the facilitator and agree on it before you start. This is part of staying in charge of your own process. (See Process 28, *Strategic planning*.)

HIGHER PURPOSE

It is useful in personal and work relationships to consider the possibility of having a higher purpose. It is also useful for you as an individual to do this. What is your higher purpose? What is the higher purpose of your relationships and your business? (See Process 42, *Finding the higher purpose*.)

VALUES

Our beliefs give birth to values that indicate what is important to us. Values are implicit in everything we do. They can be deduced from our actions. Clarifying values can be difficult. Ask yourself: Why am I doing this? Why is it important? Values are our most important driving force, yet often we are unaware of what they are. It is sometimes easier to deduce them in others than to uncover our own.

Our own values are often different from those of the people with whom we work. It is possible to work on a project with someone with very different values, as long as the values are not directly opposed. For example: You may be working on a project because you believe in its worth as a contribution to others; I may be working on a project because I believe doing so will increase my skills. Because there is no opposition between our values, we may work together productively.

However, because our values are not aligned, we may have difficulty resolving conflicts when they arise. It is useful, therefore, to address values when formulating a project, exploring how they are different and whether the differences will get in the way. Write down these values. If values are closely aligned there is likely to be a better focus, greater clarity and a stronger basis for resolving conflicts.

Values on their own are of limited usefulness. They become important when we take them out of our heads and apply them to behavior. Then they become *operational* or *applied values*. They become observable and can be challenged. For example, if I say I believe in respecting individual difference but allow little opportunity for others to be different, I can be challenged on this point. By being challenged I might learn something. I will get an opportunity to become more congruent in my behavior with my stated beliefs.

As humans we tend to be wonderfully incongruent. We seem blissfully unaware of many of our incongruities, so it is useful to bring some rigor to bear on this subject. After all, this is the basis of integrity—the state of being whole, entire or undiminished. And we have found that integrity is the basis of personal power.

ETHICS

One way to address operational values is to develop a code of ethics. Ethics relate to moral standards of behavior. They are a philosophically congruent statement of beliefs and values. We all have personal values, but we may not have made them explicit before. Writing them down in a philosophically congruent way gives us a code of ethics.

A code of ethics is developed by uncovering what our values really are as distinct from what we would like them to be. They need to be real, not a smoke screen. A code of ethics is a formal way of advising others what standards of behavior to expect from you. A code of ethics can be a helpful operational framework for peer organizations.

When you have a code of ethics you can be challenged about them, and behavior that is incongruent can be called *unethical*. This creates accountability. Ethics in business are becoming more important now because they give the public a clear basis for challenging a company's motives or actions.

Business ethics are even becoming a national and international issue. So are the relationships between business and government. Governments are increasingly being pressured to concern themselves with ethical issues—the protection of irreplaceable natural resources, the cleanliness of the air, the removal of poisons from our food and water, the protection of indigenous people, the banning of nuclear weapons. United Nations' instruments, such as the Ottawa Charter and Agenda 21, are gaining importance also.

Page 52 contains one example of an ethical code.

Code of Ethics

Respect for truth and the public's right to information are overriding principles for all journalists. In pursuance of these principles, journalists commit themselves to ethical and professional standards. All members of the Union engaged in gathering, transmitting, disseminating and commenting on news and information shall observe the following Code of Ethics in their professional activities:

a) They shall report and interpret the news with scrupulous honesty by striving to disclose all essential facts and by not suppressing relevant, available facts or distorting by wrong or improper emphasis.

b) They shall not place unnecessary emphasis on gender, race, sexual preference, religious belief, marital status or physical or mental disability.

c) In all circumstances they shall respect all confidences received in the course of their occupation.

d) They shall not allow personal interests to influence them in their professional duties.

e) They shall not allow their professional duties to be influenced by any consideration, gift or advantage offered and, where appropriate, shall disclose any such offer.

f) They shall not allow advertising or commercial considerations to influence them in their professional duties.

g) They shall use fair and honest means to obtain news, pictures, films, tapes and documents.

h) They shall identify themselves and their employers before obtaining any interview for publication or broadcast.

i) They shall respect private grief and personal privacy and shall have the right to resist the compulsion to intrude on them.

j) They shall do their utmost to correct any published or broadcast information found to be harmfully inaccurate.

A breach of this Code shall be a breach of the Union's rules and thus may give rise to disciplinary procedures under the rules. If a member is dismissed from employment or otherwise disadvantaged by an employer, and a breach of the Code is claimed and substantiated as a ground for the employer's action, the Union may decline to pursue a personal grievance on behalf of the member.

CULTURE-SETTING

A more informal way to address operational values is to develop a culture statement. *Culture-setting* is about consciously deciding how you will work together as a group. Rather than drag all your unconscious expectations about others into your work, you can design your own group's culture. The culture statement is a way of helping you live your values. It doesn't have to involve rules. You could use an inspirational statement of the ideal working environment you plan to create together. (See Process 21, *Culture-setting*.)

MANAGEMENT ALIGNMENT

The purpose of management systems, procedures and practices is to support what we do by providing clarity, order and consistency—in short, some structure. Much has been written on management systems, so we will not cover them in this book. We will say that these systems exist to make things easy and workable for everyone involved. But beware of using systems as a way of confusing or oppressing one another.

The larger the organization, the more systems are invented. Keep checking to see you have only the systems you need. The KISS principle is a good one to go by: *Keep It Super Simple.*

ATTUNEMENT

We call methods used to bring the energies of a group into balance and harmony "attuning" or "attunements." Activities that attune a group include prayer, meditation, singing or listening to music, and sleeping. Consciously breathing together and holding hands are also helpful methods. If these activities seem alien or inappropriate, there are other techniques that will help.

One we use a lot is called *Getting present.* (See Process 19.) In our business, we use a range of other processes for creating and maintaining alignment. (See Processes 16 to 32.) We like Processes 20, *Creation meeting,* 23, *Sharing withholds,* and 25, *Completion meeting,* in particular.

Conflict

*One must have chaos in order to give birth to a
dancing star.*

—*NIETZSCHE*

We will not agree or be aligned all the time. Sometimes we will disagree
a lot. Disagreement is part of decision-making, and it can also be part of a
wider harmony. Disagreement may also lead to conflict. But we need to
remember conflict is normal—it is part of life.

All relationships involve differences. We have different beliefs, different
values, different opinions, different behaviors and different areas and
thresholds of distress. We may not be able to accommodate one another's
differences or allow one another to be the way we are. We may try to
change one another and, when this doesn't work, we withdraw either
completely or in part (for example, emotionally).

When we work with others we may not be able to withdraw. We may
be faced every day with someone who has behaviors and opinions that
annoy or upset us, or trigger some other reaction from us. Let's be realistic:
Conflict is quite likely.

We have discussed issues surrounding power and alignment already.
When addressed, these issues will help resolve some areas of conflict. But
what do you do when conflict continues anyway?

WORKING WITH CONFLICT

If you do not attend to conflict it can lead to resentment, lack of cooperation, lack of energy, people avoiding one another, indirect attacks, subversion and ultimately violence or war.

Lack of conflict in the workplace doesn't mean it is necessarily a healthy environment. It may indicate apathy, lack of commitment, boredom, lack of safety (the personal risk involved for disagreeing is seen to be too high) or low self-esteem. A highly creative workplace is likely to have a higher degree of conflict than others.

Most of us are scared of open conflict and avoid it if we can. There is some risk involved in expressing and working through conflict. If the working through involves harsh words and name-calling, people can feel deeply hurt. Relationships can be damaged, sometimes permanently. Some people are afraid that, if they start to express their anger, they may go out of control and become violent, or that others may do this. These fears may be based on personal experience.

So why take the risk? Why not avoid conflict at all costs? Conflict is a little like disease—prevention is best. That means it is wise to attend to areas in which disagreements may occur *before* they become an issue. If you have not prevented a conflict from happening, your next choice is to "treat" it early, or hope it goes away. If it goes away over time, fine. If it doesn't, then you will still have to handle (treat) it. By then, however, the problem is likely to have grown more serious.

Anger and upset over the same things, over and over, is usually about our being attached to something—a belief or an idea—and attached to being right about it. We think what we believe is the truth. This becomes more important than being with another person, which would involve allowing each of us to be different.

Zenergy, our small company, is largely made up of facilitators. Naturally we are very interested in process. But we don't always agree on which process to use or how to implement it. We can take very different positions about it! Sometimes several people propose different things and each one believes he or she is right. When we get "positional," our enlightened thinking tends to go out the window.

KEEP COMMUNICATING

We have found it is important to say what is not working for us and to keep talking about it. When we stop communicating, we start to withdraw emotionally from one another. We withhold ourselves. The relationship dies a little. A helpful credo is "Communicate or die."

EXAMPLE: For Christmas, David gave Dale a vase that she didn't like. She felt awkward because David was often at her place. Rather than hide it, she worked up the courage to tell David how she felt. He was able to arrange for her to exchange it for another style.

EXAMPLE: David felt left out of two decisions that had been made and also felt Anne was not treating him as an equal. He finally spoke up and said what he felt. He was listened to. Anne agreed to monitor how she was behaving toward David.

Communicate, even when it is hard, because this is the key to resolving most conflicts. Skills are involved. These are known as *assertion skills*:

- Being able to express what is happening and how we feel about it in a non-blaming way

- Being able to hear criticism and respond to it without becoming defensive

- Being willing to negotiate toward a workable solution without compromising ourselves

The following open-ended statements can be useful to promote assertiveness. Fill them in with your own comments: "When you do ____, I feel ____. I request that you ____." These kinds of assertion skills are always useful; but using them takes practice.

More and more, we (the authors) find it important to tell each other what is bothering or upsetting us. Sometimes what we say can sound harsh to others. But we have found this skill is necessary to stay in a whole, honest relationship with one another. (See Process 23, *Sharing withholds*.)

LET IT OUT

Sometimes it is wonderful just to shout at one another and clear the air. This can change the energy and enable both of you to see a new way out of your impasse. Sometimes we see just how ridiculous we are being. Do you know how to do this, or is it too scary? You may have had experiences from the past, particularly in childhood, that make this method disturbing to try. Practice shouting on your own at first if it is hard for you—perhaps in the car when you are driving by yourself. Then agree to practice with another person in a safe environment. This can be liberating. You may want to take turns. Make sure you both feel safe and are not personally threatened by yelling.

Wouldn't it be great if all workplaces had "raging rooms" where you could go, yell and punch cushions? Some workplaces in Japan have rooms with effigies of the bosses that the staff can punch to their hearts' content.

STUCK PATTERNS

The hardest conflicts to solve, we find, are the ones where one person's "stuck pattern" sets off the other's "stuck pattern"—a kind of reaction pattern occurs that goes in circles until it is interrupted.

EXAMPLE: Dale complains to Anne about something she has or has not done. Anne gets defensive. David jumps to her aid (rescues her) although he knows the criticism is valid. Dale feels unheard and silenced. They all feel upset. This pattern was finally identified and named. Now the pattern is out in the open and can be interrupted by any one of the three people involved.

If the same behavior happens more than twice, a pattern is in there somewhere! See if you can spot it together. In our case, we now have a "pattern-buster" system, and we all look for patterns to break.

We all get stuck at times. Don't beat yourself up when you are annoyed, angry or upset. It only adds to the pain. Allow yourself to feel angry or hurt. When you are ready, say, "I feel upset. I feel hurt. I feel unheard."

We are all vulnerable underneath. It can be hard to allow ourselves to be vulnerable and to let others see that we are vulnerable. Can you be with your own "hurt child"? Can you make it safe for this child to speak? Can you be with another person's hurt child and allow that child space to cry, speak and just be? (See also chapter 12, *Peer counseling*.)

It's liberating to be around people who don't get caught up in other people's emotional stuff. Can you allow someone else to be grumpy for a while, and just let him be? Some of us are just grumpy from time to time. Do you feel you have to make it better or feel that the mood must have something to do with you?

STRONG REACTIONS

Sometimes we don't get along too well with someone. The person is OK but we just don't warm up to him or her. It happens. If we react strongly to someone, positively or negatively, and the person pushes our buttons a lot, you can bet other stuff is happening "behind the scenes" as well. Some trigger in that person's behavior is taking us back to our past, usually childhood. This makes it hard to let go of the annoyance, anger or fear. Or, the person may remind us of someone in particular from our past, perhaps in appearance, voice or mannerisms. In such circumstances an identity check can help sort things out. (See Process 35, *Identity check*, and chapter 12, *Peer counseling*.)

CONFLICT WHEN WE WANT CONSENSUS

Although optimistically we believe there is always a way forward that will lead to agreement, it is important to recognize that the possibility also exists that agreement will not be reached. Whatever transpires, individual differences of view need to be honored and celebrated. (See "Underpinning values," pages 8 to 10.)

That said, what can be done when we genuinely need to reach agreement and we are poles apart? Here are some suggestions:

- Allow the person most concerned to make the decision. Perhaps you can agree together on some guidelines.

- Leave the decision for later, or take a break.

- Lead an energizer activity or a five-minute laugh, in which everyone laughs (or hums if they can't laugh).

- Ask everyone to argue convincingly the point of view they like the least.

- Break down the decision. Identify what you can align on and see what points of disagreement are left.

- Identify the assumptions and beliefs underlying the issue. Get to the heart of the matter. (See chapter 15, *Peer inquiry*, "strategic dialog," page 132.)

- Have everyone sit in a circle. Let each person speak in turn. After one round, see if you have uncovered a way to move the discussion forward. If not, have another round. After that, the solution will be clear, or you will realize the issue has changed.

- Imagine what will happen in six months, a year, five years' time if you don't agree. How important is the decision now?

- Meditate together.

- Go for a walk, a drive or to a café together as a way of building your relationships before addressing the issue again.

- Request everyone to "get off it!"—that is, drop their positional stances.

- Put all the possibilities into a hat and pull one out. Agree in advance to this solution.

- Use the holonomic principle. (See Process 42, *Finding the higher purpose.*)

- Do something together that feels dangerous, such as taking a roller-coaster ride. In the scary moments, consider your attachment to your point of view.

- Give up being right.

- Bring in a facilitator.

- Ask an elder or spiritual mentor for help.

- Train in effective meeting and facilitation skills.

Models for running a business meeting are given in Processes 60 and 61. Processes for resolving conflicts are provided in Processes 33 to 40.

USING A FACILITATOR

If your group or organization is unable to work through conflicts productively, or if similar issues keep coming up, it can be helpful to call in a professional facilitator who is trained in conflict-resolution techniques.

TRAINING

Facilitator training programs are available in many countries. Our company, Zenergy, runs training programs in a number of countries. You can contact us by e-mail: zenergy@xtra.co.nz (you may also enjoy reading our book, *The Art of Facilitation*).

Spirituality

*If work is all about doing, then the soul
is all about being: the indiscriminate
enjoyer of everything that comes our way.
If work is the world, then the soul is our home.*

—DAVID WHYTE

What is the place of spirituality in the work environment? If spirituality is a part of whole being, can we keep it out of the workplace?

What is meant by "spirituality"? Our definition for spirituality is *the capacity to connect with the sacred and the divine.* How might this be expressed at work? Purpose, sacred space, ritual and by bringing the sacred to everyday activities are some ways we know of.

Industrialized work has, on the whole, been concerned with the materialistic and the pragmatic. Spirituality was usually kept separate from work and was mainly expressed through organized religion. Christianity observed Sunday as a day of rest, a non-work day. Christian values of honesty, fairness and service were practiced by some.

The split between the material and divine was mirrored in the secularization of work. The idea of divine purpose—work as a sacred activity, a calling, a vocation—lost ground. Artists, teachers, ministers and doctors still had vocations, but most people had jobs, careers and professions. They worked, played and worshiped as separate activities.

Looking at this idea from the concept of being a whole person, we need to reconsider this split. A sense of the sacred and the divine cannot be separated artificially from different parts of life. An integrated life means all parts of our life are affected by all aspects of our being.

Taking this concept further, human life is but one part of the fabric of life in our world, which includes other life forms—animal, vegetable and mineral. We are part of a greater whole. And the world is part of an even greater whole—the universe, the cosmos.

What implications does this have for the work in which we are involved and how we approach it? Does it affect how we go about business? Does it affect the kind of work in which we are willing to be involved? What we find is that the purpose of our work, the usefulness of it, the effect it has on the community and the environment, the values and ethics embodied in it, all need to be appraised.

Perhaps it is time we tuned in again to the sacred in work and play as part of our whole lives. The divine connection is not only for individual nourishment, but also for the collective—the communities of people who make up organizations and businesses.

LIFE PURPOSE

What is your individual life purpose? Do you have a sense of this? Is it relevant to you to have one? If it is relevant, how do you apply this purpose to your work? How does your individual purpose fit with the organizational purpose of your work? Is there an alignment? Do you see this as an integrity issue—that you work in a way that honors your individual purpose?

Does your work organization have a purpose? What is it? Is it to make a profit for shareholders? If so, how do you feel about this? Who are the shareholders and what are they doing with the fruits of your labor? Have you thought about this?

If your work has a practical purpose (to produce a product for a specific market), does it also have a higher purpose—a sacred purpose of which the practical purpose is a part? The purpose in our company, Zenergy, is to create new ways of working together. Our vision is to create a quantum shift in world consciousness to the point we will live cooperatively as one community.

How does your organization relate to and affect the environment, the community, the world? Raising these questions can appear rather "heavy." You may wonder if you really need to think about such things. However, for us as authors to be congruent in our approach with this book, we must raise these issues.

SACRED SPACE

By "sacred space," we mean a place in which you can remember and connect into that which you consider spiritual and divine. Are there any sacred spaces in your home? You may think of them as special places or spots rather than as sacred. A meditation space, perhaps, or a garden where you can go for quiet "being" time. Or you may have an altar or shelf with special (sacred) objects on it—stones, leaves, whatever means something to you.

What about in your workplace? What is sacred space there? Is there a quiet room or garden? Or are the sacred places related more to the board-room or director's chair or car? Do you have a sacred spot in your office? Think about what really is sacred in your workplace.

RITUAL

What rituals do you practice? You certainly have some. Are they all related to what is practical—washing, shaving, brushing teeth, eating breakfast, tidying your workspace? Or are some of them sacred rituals—meditation, prayer, lighting candles, chanting, dancing? Of course, all your rituals can be sacred if you want them to be, just by bringing your awareness of them to bear.

What work rituals are you aware of? Do you always start the day and finish the same way? Does tea or coffee in the morning provide an opportunity for a ritual gathering of work colleagues? Are there rituals around receiving your pay?

We have rituals in our Zenergy workspace. We have weekly "creation" meetings on Monday morning and "completion" meetings on Friday afternoon. Whoever is in the office takes part. Quite often, those of us in other places will phone in to "get complete" at the end of a week or to find out what our theme for the following week will be, which we decide during our creation meetings.

We also have rituals around our weekly business meeting. We check in and "get present" at the start of it and have an "attunement" exercise (See page 188). We "get complete" at the end of it. Morning tea and muffins are also something of a ritual for us.

It is fun to begin to notice rituals and treat them as sacred moments. It is also useful to design rituals that highlight who you are being at work. Try it—rituals can make a big difference. (See Processes 20, *Creation meeting;* 24, *Getting complete;* 31, *Ritual;* and 61, *Zenergy business-meeting model.*)

THE SACRED IN EVERY MOMENT

We have a favorite Zen saying: "Before enlightenment drawing water, chopping wood; after enlightenment drawing water, chopping wood."

Everyday activities continue, no matter how enlightened we may be. The opportunity, though, is to bring the awareness, the mindfulness, the being of enlightenment through into every daily activity and illuminate it with presence. From a Christian perspective, this may be explained as recognizing "Christ's presence" in everything—seeing your whole life as a prayer to the divine.

Dale doesn't like housework much. She took on the morning routine of dishes, however, and cleaning became a spiritual practice—bringing awareness to bear. It changed everything. Every movement became important, every sound; the dish water became a sacred pool and the dishes were purified and squeaked with delight.

You may want to try bringing your full awareness to aspects of your work. Start with something specific and then extend it—your life will transform daily.

Every moment of every day is an opportunity for being to express itself (living moment by moment). All of life can be a sacred journey and every step a sacred step.

TRANSCENDENCE

Are there opportunities for transcendence to occur in your life? Are there spaces for this to happen? It could be a walk in the park or garden, watching a sunrise, sunset, the wilderness, the stars, children; breathing, being in the bath, being with a lover or loved one, being with a new idea or image. Do you provide space for exaltation and glorious moments?

Do you have magic moments at work when you step into glory—when you connect with others in a magical way? Are there moments when you connect with the subtle psychic realms and see auras and energy patterns, or symbols, patterns and messages? Does your spirit fly?

Bringing the full awareness of two or more people together can be a powerful experience. Try this with a friend—with eye contact and in silence: Become empty and aware. Bring that awareness together by being together, both fully present; two mirrors. It is a magical space of creation in which you need to utter anything that comes up. It is a sacred space.

PERSONAL PRESENCE

Your innate spirituality can be made manifest through your personal presence. John Heron (*Group Facilitation*, 1993) talks of "the ability to be empowered by one's own inner resources, the wellspring within, and thereby to elicit empowerment in others." He sees this as available through training in the conscious use of your physical posture and as "the birthright of every person who takes the trouble to practice it." He talks of being "rather like the original light of the soul taking charge of its earthly location and its human relationships."

In an interview in our book *The Art of Facilitation*, Heron talked about

allowing some immanent power within to shape your unique expression . . . There's an inner source, what Jean Houston calls a Godseed, *an* entelechy *self. This is a* wellspring or *personal potential, and it's an accessible mystery. All you have to do is stand up and feel the whole of your gesture in space, feel your presence within the world, and you're open to this wellspring.*

The role of the spiritual guide

Do you have a person to whom you look as a spiritual guide—a flesh-and-blood guide or an other-world guide? You may want to consider having a workplace spiritual guide or focus also. We enjoy giving this role to one of our members who is also a healer. He does not consider himself different from the rest of us, but we enjoy bestowing this status on him. He is our *kaumatua,* our elder. He provides a focus, an everyday reminder of the importance of our own spirituality.

A sacred project

Do you have a special sacred project—something that involves a quest, a journey, internal or external?

Many businesses see relationships with charitable organizations as an integral part of their work. The relationship can have a special meaning or significance in line with the vision of the company, so it is not a marketing tool, and it may or may not be made public. A New Zealand company, Self Heal, adapts New Zealand plants to the principles of European herbalism. It gives 10% of everything it sells to a religious order, the Sisters of Compassion. The founder, Sister Suzanne Aubert, worked closely with the indigenous Maori people, using her botanical knowledge to make herbal medicines. Many Self Heal products are based on Sister Aubert's recipes. In addition, one of Self Heal's co-directors had three children with disabilities who went to a school run by the sisters.

Our *kaumatua's* sacred project

Leonard Jeffs, our Zenergy *kaumatua,* is of Tongan, Samoan and Maori descent. He has an intuitive urge to produce an audiotape of the natural sounds of the New Zealand bush together with ancient Polynesian music and chants. This could be used during meditation to raise consciousness of the importance of indigenous peoples and their spiritual affinity with the land.

> *I envisage this tape with Polynesian flutes, the sea or running water and maybe a* tui *and a bell bird, and ancient chants about the creation and*

"Tihei Mauriora," and highlighting the commonality of the region—evoking the common thread of the "creation" throughout the Polynesian triangle [Hawaii across to Easter Island and down to New Zealand].

It will be an acknowledgment of the future as here-and-now and the process of acculturation. When people get together and pay homage and respect to Mother Earth—the land—they become attuned to the harmonies of the Earth and nature.

It is inclusive, for we are all people of the Earth and, indeed, the only thing that is constant is nature itself—we breathe the same air, are bathed by the same wind and rain. This is the one thing that is consistent for us all.

It is important to pay respect to the tangata whenua—the people of the land of the region, the indigenous people—to recognize their status and particular affinity with the land. It is part of paying respect to nature itself—they are the guardians of the land.

When people get together, it is important to acknowledge behind the eyes, beyond the physical, we are only balls of energy—thought and spirit—this is all that comprises the human ethos. The energetic body is less tangible and much larger than the physical body.

MORE THOUGHTS ON THE SPIRITUAL

Here are some more thoughts on the spiritual from Len:

The spiritual is not intellectual—it is a state of being, it is an exalted state of existence.

In the human existence, energy can be either positive or negative. Sometimes it is easier to take on negative thoughts. This is actually a waste of energy. So what we do with it—where we put it—is always a choice.

When we move into the next dimension—state of existence—all we take with us is our positive energy—a parcel of accumulated knowledge—that's all. So the choices we make now are important because we are preparing for another journey. We can reap the positive here in the present to take with us to the next dimension.

It is important for the Earth to be clean and harmonious. We are all now reconnecting to our true selves through the medium of the Earth. Collectively we can share positive energy—creating synergy. We become magnets for this energy and a big magnet of aligned people becomes a huge magnet drawing in lots more positive energy.

In Zenergy, it is important for us to be aligned and attuned, to expand and develop so we can generate more positive energy. Aligned positive energy can dissipate negative energy. Aligned energy—positive energy—opens the psyche and brings up what needs to be healed—this is the dissipation of negative energy.

Healing is done by yourself. Other people can facilitate it, but the final decision must be yours.

The shadow side

We may think we are in the meeting room to preserve our job and our career, while at bottom the soul is making another bid for first-hand experience through courageous speech. It has no interest in being right; it simply intuits another life . . . Folded in on itself by our strategies for survival, it is trying to open. As Rilke said: "Where I am folded in upon myself, there I am a lie."

—DAVID WHYTE

The shadow represents the parts of ourselves, our relationships, our organizations and our communities that are unconscious or unaccepted, and in need of integration. The shadow lives in the folds, the parts of ourselves that are unseen and unknown—the aspects to which we do not have access or which we do not want to own through fear of rejection by others. We often reject parts of ourselves rather than face possible rejection by others.

The shadow side is part of existence—light supposes dark, just as long supposes short. As we look deeply and fiercely into the folds and shadows, we see and are able to bring out these unconscious parts and shed light on them. This process is part of becoming a mature human being. The shadow parts that are brought forward and integrated enhance our personal power. The shadow parts that are rejected or repressed deplete our personal power and have power over us. They show up in addictive and unconscious ways that dominate and deaden us both individually and collectively.

Groups, organizations, communities and nations all have shadow sides. It takes effort and courage to acknowledge and bring out the shadow parts and subject them to the light of consciousness. In the process of bringing out the shadow side there is always a lot of resistance. It is as if the shadow wants to hang on to its own and remain secret. Sometimes the shadow presents itself as an enormous and insoluble problem. We feel it could overwhelm us. Bringing it out into the open feels a little like dying. However, once the problem is named, spoken and shared, the heat seems to go out of it. It becomes less potent and more able to be worked through.

At other times the shadow presents itself as a little worry that seems hardly important enough to name and share. Unfortunately it may be the tip of an iceberg that needs to be fully explored and unfrozen. Naming the worry may encourage others to share their concerns, and the underlying issues will emerge.

When we started to write this chapter we were at a meeting in Taupo, New Zealand. We were working on a laptop computer using a portable power source. We wrote a couple of pages and were quite inspired by our writing, which was flowing beautifully. Suddenly the screen went blank. Nothing we did could revive it. The screen came up after a few minutes but we had lost the whole piece—we had forgotten to save it.

We reflected on the incident, which upset us quite a bit. It was hard to reconstruct the ideas with quite the same flow. In our enthusiasm we had become unconscious about the need to save the material. It was as if the shadow side had taken advantage of our "unconscious" state and reclaimed the material back into the void. The shadow does not like to be exposed to the light. Perhaps it was resisting our efforts to unmask it.

It also reminded us of the dynamic and organic nature of writing. This book had begun to take on a life of its own. It was beginning to assert itself and make known its own preferences and needs. It had started to interact with us and guide us.

The second time we worked on this chapter was on Waiheke Island during a storm. There was a power failure and all the power on the island went off for a number of hours. The battery on the laptop continued to operate and, as it got dark, we lit a candle to see the keyboard. We read the part about the power surge at Tauhara and quickly saved what we had written to avoid another disaster.

In the same way, the shadow side teaches and guides us to reveal ourselves to ourselves and to others. This creates depth, richness and integrity in ourselves, in our relationships and in our projects. You might say that the whole work of the world is to become conscious and that, as this happens, we are freed to respond on all levels, both individually and collectively. We become free and responsive personally, interpersonally, socially, politically and globally.

THE SHADOW SIDE OF CO-OPERATION

One part of the shadow side of co-operation is seen when we co-operate (conform) with others at the expense of our own good. We compromise our own autonomy for the group. This is rarely a good choice. It tends to backfire. We tend to feel resentful, even used, if we do things that go against our best interests.

Co-operation for this reason is not about compromising yourself. That doesn't work. Co-operation is about becoming more and more aware of our own beliefs and values, and bringing them with us when we are working on a collective issue with others.

Full co-operation requires a full sense of individual autonomy and the ability to stand up for one's own authentic wants. This requires a high level of self-awareness (self-connection), as well as a strong desire to connect with others. It also requires the ability to recognize and appreciate the authentic wants of others. ("Authentic" can be defined only by the person it concerns; it's coercive to impose "authenticity" on someone else.) The creative tension between autonomy and collective action is the essence of full co-operation.

The shadow side of autonomy is a tendency toward self-absorption, willfulness, stubbornness and isolation. These tendencies need to be countered by a willingness and opportunity to interact creatively with others.

INDIVIDUAL SHADOW

To work with the shadow individually takes courage. You may want to work with a counselor. The shadow indicates itself in addictions, obsessions and patterned behavior. It may also express itself in vague longings, a continuing lack of energy and depression. These behaviors hide our authentic, denied hurts and needs. Perhaps we were never encouraged to be ourselves or express an exuberance for life.

It helps to begin to uncover where our patterned behavior comes from. What do we really believe? Often these beliefs come from childhood or from our first work experiences.

Notice when you feel uptight and uncomfortable. Ask yourself: Why do I feel this way? What beliefs are at work here? Did I choose them, or are they old, conditioned responses? Once we uncover the old, conditioned beliefs we can choose to change them. It takes rigor and a certain fearlessness to do this. Once you do uncover them, however, you can choose new beliefs. As a result, the behavior based on those old responses will change, too.

EXAMPLE: Dale noticed that she often felt uptight when others were late or forgot things at work. The tension she felt seemed to be out of proportion to the incident. She began to look at what was happening— where the tension came from and what the beliefs were that seemed to trigger it. She realized that in her first career as a professional musician she had established a strong set of beliefs. These beliefs were still influencing her. Her training at that time dictated that being late and forgetting things (instrument, music) were entirely unacceptable for a professional musician. Indeed, without strong habits in these areas one would never be hired . . . and so one would never get to work with other professionals.

She had identified the source of her intolerance. It was obvious. Her colleagues would not be acceptable in an orchestra! Hence the tension. Having identified the system of beliefs at work, Dale was able to introduce newer, more appropriate ones. And at the same time she influenced others to be more sensitive to the clock and to come to meetings better prepared.

THE GROUP SHADOW

GROUP-THINK

Another aspect of the shadow side is the phenomenon of "group-think." In group-think, the good feelings of uniqueness and belonging we find in a group, community or nation lead us to believe that our uniqueness means we are better than someone else or some other group. We objectify others and turn them into things rather than recognizing them as persons as individual as ourselves. Group-think is the basis of all "isms"—racism, sexism, ageism, homophobia. It is also a basis of war—we must objectify other groups as the "enemy" to be able to kill them.

PEER PRESSURE

Group-think leads to another difficulty—peer pressure. This comes from wanting to be part of the group and conform to group norms. We become vulnerable to peer pressure. We are tempted to act in ways that keep us in good standing with the group. Peer pressure threatens personal integrity. Resist peer pressure—watch out for and be the guardian of your integrity! It is an integral element of personal power.

WALKING AROUND BROKEN GLASS

Another common shadow pattern of groups is avoidance—refusal to see or "own" the problem. We call this "walking around broken glass." Everyone colludes in picking their way around the issue, pretending it isn't there or hoping it will go away if it is ignored. It is also the emperor's-new-clothes phenomenon. In that old fable, everyone knows the emperor is naked when he parades through the town in his new "clothes," but no one will risk saying so.

Group collusion is the problem here. Someone needs to be brave enough to name the unacknowledged issue and break the silence. Once named, the issue can come into the light and be addressed. A facilitator can help the group create a safe space to address the specific issue or "broken glass."

PATTERNED BEHAVIOR AND SABOTAGE

Patterned behavior is hard enough to interrupt on an individual basis. It's even stickier when a number of patterns trigger one another in a group. (See chapter 6, *Conflict*.)

Patterned behavior often sabotages ourselves and others. We undermine our own and the group's brilliance through unconscious or semi-conscious patterns. We arrive late, don't meet our commitments, stop listening, judge and "kill off" one another mentally. What is behind these behaviors, to which we all are prone? Perhaps we cannot bear the thought of being successful or being fully connected to others. That condition may be just too unknown and scary. We know how to be separate, alone and different, and we don't know about being with others in a powerful way. It may feel like dying. We may lose our understanding of ourselves: "Help, my identity may be lost." So we cling to old behaviors rather than take the leap into a new way of being. (See Process 45, *Exploring the group's shadow*.)

THE ORGANIZATION SHADOW

Uncovering the shadow in the workplace takes a certain mental rigor. Notice what patterns and behaviors annoy people or shut them down. These patterns need to be brought into the open. An outside facilitator can help here. The facilitator can provide suggestions for interrupting the patterns as the group uncovers them.

Common patterns in the workplace include being stuck in power/powerlessness patterns, indecisiveness, insensitivity, unwillingness to trust others, not following through on commitments, not speaking up, feeling resigned about things not working, squabbling about money and talking behind the backs of others.

You will need a safe environment to uncover the shadow. It's hard to "speak the unspeakable" out loud. The irony is that speaking the unspeakable is more for the person speaking than for the person to whom it is spoken. The reaction is often stronger for the person speaking: "Wow! Did I really have the guts to say that?" The person to whom the comment has been directed is typically not as concerned or upset.

Once patterns like these are brought into the open, the whole group can look for the beliefs underpinning the comments. Then everyone can take some responsibility for introducing new beliefs and interrupting the patterns.

What shadow issues are you aware of in your community?
What shadow issues are you aware of in your country?

SHADOW AND SOCIETY

The shadow is always active at a wider community and national level. It is easier to recognize the shadow as issues come to light. For example, incest, domestic violence and child abuse were shadow issues before they were brought into wider social awareness. Before then, they were hidden in the shadows, not spoken about and even, as in domestic violence, not recognized by the law.

In New Zealand, taking land from the Maori people was sanctioned by law—the issue existed in the shadows and was justified through various arguments. The annihilation of indigenous peoples in Australia, the United States and other countries is part of the shadow side of nations.

Political correctness is related to group-think. Ideas become beliefs for a majority or dominant group in society. When these ideas gain acceptance, they are perceived as the "truth," and there is little room for people to express opposing ideas. Political correctness can become oppressive and limiting.

THINKING POINTS

What do you see as shadow issues in the world at this time?

WORLD SHADOW

There are many world views. Can we allow different ones to exist concurrently? Are some world views too dangerous to be allowed to exist? Is there a right way? What about issues such as world hunger, unequal distribution of resources, pollution, environmental destruction, nuclear war? Are these part of the world shadow?

Perhaps one shadow issue in the world is the "tyranny of absolutes"; that is, people supposing their beliefs are the truth or that any set of beliefs can represent the absolute truth. This idea is at the bottom of spiritual oppression and religious wars.

Applying Co-operacy

Team

There are many kinds of teams: sports teams, work teams, project teams.

A team was probably the first grouping you thought of when considering peer relationships and co-operacy.

What is a team? A team is a group of people who need one another in order to achieve a common goal. It is a co-operative structure. A team suggests a sense of belonging, commitment and motivation—an aligned, focused and intentional group. "We are a team!" We are united and purposeful.

Once Dale and Anne did an informal survey on an airplane flying between Auckland, New Zealand, and Melbourne, Australia—a four-hour flight. They asked most of the passengers what a "team" meant to them. What was noticeable was not so much the detail of the answers but how everyone wanted to respond and seemed to know lots about "teams." Everyone had been on or was on a team. All age groups were animated talking about teams. Sports teams were high on the list, but so were work teams, the armed services and various group activities.

GROUP INTELLIGENCE

A team is a form of group intelligence. Problems are often so complex that they cannot be solved by individuals. A team of individuals with different skills and experience can learn together—become a learning organism, a group intelligence. Peter Senge, writing in *The Fifth Discipline*, names team learning as one of the five disciplines necessary for an effective organization.

DISTINCTIONS OF TEAM

"Teams" can be described in many ways. Here are some we value:

PURPOSE

A team is necessary only if you are up to something—a game or a project. There is no team without a project that requires more than one person to fulfill it. The team is a group of resources for accomplishing something.

VISION

A team needs a vision. What is the vision that the project is part of fulfilling? This is what will inspire the team when the going gets tough. Draw or write the vision on a big sheet of paper and post it in a prominent place. Maybe your group's vision is a song or a poem.

MEMBERSHIP

Who is in the team? Who isn't? A team requires clear boundaries. In some situations, the team comprises the best possible people available to fulfill needed roles. In other cases the team comprises anyone who is willing to go for it—to be committed to the team purpose and vision, and who is willing to train to be the best he or she can be. How are team members decided upon? Is the team self-selecting, or are members chosen? If chosen, by whom?

OWNERSHIP

Team members become part of the team and own the team project. They identify strongly with the team. The success of the New Zealand America's Cup campaign in 1995 was attributed to the sailors' involvement in the design of the boat and in operational decisions. This enabled the crew to feel they were sailing their "own" boat.

RESULTS

A team is about producing results of some kind. A hot team has a powerful relationship to results. They enjoy getting results—victory, winning. "Winning" is achieving the promised results. This can be a positive side of competition.

STRUCTURE FOR FULFILLMENT

A team needs a clear action plan to fulfill when working on a project. Review the action plan regularly. Everyone can contribute input into the plan, and everyone needs to agree. A team keeps track of its commitments and projected results in a tangible way—written down where they can be seen frequently as a reminder, rather than in someone's head. Use lots of charts!

COORDINATED ACTION

Team members have to be most concerned with achieving *team* results rather than individual glory. Team members need to be willing to dance together. They need to be able to play and pass the ball. When individuals in it are aligned, the team is a bigger, stronger whole than it can be otherwise. (See chapter 5, *Alignment.*)

INTEGRITY

A team rises or falls on its integrity, which is about being honest with yourself and others. Integrity is about giving and honoring your word—doing what you say you are going to do. It is learning to listen to your own truth and hearing the truth of others, which may be very different from your own. It is about understanding your own limits and knowing when and how to say no.

Integrity is also about not withholding information that could be useful to the team. It includes renegotiating quickly if you can't deliver on a promise. Discussion about unmet promises can waste time in team meetings. It is best not to attend to undelivered promises in meetings but to handle them through a decision manager outside the meeting. Integrity is honoring one another as whole beings—being loyal and not speaking disrespectfully about others behind their backs. Integrity is the source of personal power.

COMMUNICATION

A team needs to communicate within itself, especially when things are going wrong. Teams need members to say what needs to be said, to be honest and to share what they know. Team members need to see conflict as positive and bring it into the open. They must commit to open communication even when communication is hard. Acknowledgment, affirmation and encouragement are important elements of communication. (See Process 48, *Day-to-day feedback*.)

IN TRAINING

A hot team is always in training to be the best it can be. If the team has a coach, members must be willing to be coached. If your team doesn't have a coach, get one!

INTENTIONALITY

A team needs to be intentional and not waste time on side issues or poorly defined issues. Everyone must understand that the results—all of them— will be achieved.

INDIVIDUAL RESPONSIBILITY

Individuals need to be valued for their expertise and take responsibility for contributing their expertise. The team gives individuals responsibility to take action in their area of expertise. Team work is a dance of many wholes, not many halves.

HANDLING BREAKDOWNS

The team needs a process for handling breakdowns. "Breakdowns" are anything that could be better—the more breakdowns attended to, the better. (See Process 51, *Resolving breakdowns*.)

RIGOR

A sharp team will work rigorously to have the above distinctions in place at all times. Distinctions tend to fade out and need to be re-emphasized periodically. (See Process 49, *Hot team*.)

CULTURE

A team needs to be clear about how its members will work together, what values are key to the team and how they will be reflected in behaviors. These are sometimes called *operational values* or *rules of operation*. In 1995, the America's Cup-winning yachting team, Team New Zealand, used the following rules of operation:

- Fairness and honesty—"Play nicely together."
- Openness—"Share your toys."
- Emphasize simplicity.
- Focus—"Remember the big picture."
- We will encourage creativity and emphasize follow-through.

CELEBRATION

A team needs ways to mark progress and achievement. Celebration has an element of ritual about it and can include marking special moments through declaration, enjoying results and also having fun and letting off steam together. Celebration also increases intimacy.

LEADERSHIP

Leadership can arise from the team—the team recognizes its leader(s). There may be different leaders for different functions. There can be no leadership without a team. The strongest teams choose their own leaders and encourage the development of leadership in one another.

MANAGEMENT

A team can learn to manage itself. It is more important for everyone on the team to understand the fine points of management rather than for the team to have a specific manager. Management is about creating a structure for fulfilling a purpose and the systems and practices to support this. Management is about wise use of resources. Management requires action plans, displays, commitments and promises. Management is about "plugging the project into reality" so it can happen smoothly, with nothing left to chance. Management is about knowing how to relate to people. Management skills are needed by everyone in the team—to self-manage and to assist others.

Synergy

This is what a team can achieve if the above distinctions are in place.

Project management

Project management is an important body of skills. It helps to know the stages every project goes through: formulation, concentration, momentum and completion.

Formulation: The first stage of a project. The purpose, vision, objectives, team membership and culture, action plans and resources will be developed or set.

Concentration: In this stage the team will expend a lot of energy implementing and fine-tuning the action plan. This is a high-energy, "all shoulders to the wheel" time. It takes more energy to start the wheel rolling than at any other time. At this stage the group will expend high energy for small results.

Momentum: If the concentration stage has been effective, the project will gain momentum. The wheel is turning; now it must be steered. Results begin to appear. Team members begin to feel a sense of accomplishment. The success or other outcome of the project will be indicated, and time will have to be set aside for some reflection on progress.

Completion: This is the last stage of the project, when final results are collated and loose ends are tied up. Evaluations are carried out and learning is distilled so that it can be applied to the next projects. Team members give and receive acknowledgment; their successes are celebrated. The team carries out a completion ritual.

KINDS OF WORK TEAMS
You will find a variety of teams in the workplace.

PROJECT TEAM
A project team has a clear purpose, a defined set of outcomes and a finish date. People come together to fulfill the project and then move on.

SELF-DIRECTED TEAM
A self-directed team is usually an ongoing team, responsible for managing itself to achieve certain agreed-on functions. Members stay together over time.

COORDINATING TEAM
A coordinating team is made up of one or two members drawn from other teams that need to be coordinated. A coordinating team performs a management function and can replace managers in a non-hierarchical organization.

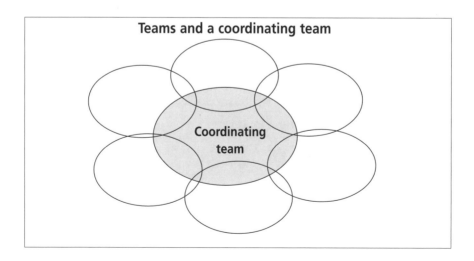

Teams and a coordinating team

Coordinating team

CROSS-FUNCTIONAL TEAM

A cross-functional team contains people drawn from different parts of an organization, with different skill sets. A cross-functional team is usually a project team. Cross-functional teams are often used to design organizational change.

SUPPORT TEAM

This is a team set up specifically to support another team or project. It contracts to carry out a support role. Sometimes it is a sub-team of a larger team.

VIRTUAL TEAM

A team in which members talk by computer and don't meet in person.

CONSENSUS DECISION-MAKING

Consensus decision-making is the usual decision-making method for teams (and co-operative organizations). Consensus decision-making is based on a commitment by all participants to reach agreement. As outlined in chapter 1, beliefs and values underpin collective decision-making. These are so important that they warrant repeating here:

- All people are intrinsically of equal worth.
- Difference is to be valued, honored and celebrated.
- It is possible for people to live and work together cooperatively.
- The best decisions are made by those people who are affected by them.

Agreement can mean any of the following:

- Everyone agrees.
- Everyone agrees to disagree.
- Some people agree and others agree to align with them.
- Everyone agrees to delegate (or empower) one or a number of participants or even an outside person to decide (usually within certain guidelines).

- Everyone agrees that only those specific persons affected by the decision will make it.
- Everyone agrees that sub-groups can make their own independent decision.
- Everyone agrees that a certain chosen percentage, perhaps 51% to 95%, will constitute agreement (as an interim measure only).
- All agree except one or two, who:

  – express their disagreement and allow the group to proceed with its decision.

  – propose alternative solutions until the group agrees.

  Note: There is no power of unmoving veto. The person who dissents, out of a commitment to reach agreement, must propose a counter-solution. All are encouraged to think creatively, outside their usual thinking patterns.
- Everyone agrees to delay the decision.
- No decision is made.

  Note: The fallback position is agreement by all—not a majority. (See Process 50, *Consensus decision-making.*)

TEAM-BASED ORGANIZATIONS

There is a move at present in many countries to incorporate teamwork into hierarchical organizations, and to shift from hierarchical to team-based organizations. Lots of different kinds of teams are being created, from short-term project teams to self-directed, ongoing teams.

A lot of books have been written on teamwork, how to set up teams, the roles people play in teams, how to choose the right people for a particular team and what to do. Some of these books are listed in the bibliography.

We believe that teamwork is something that can be created anywhere with training and coaching in the distinctions listed above.

PROBLEMS WITH TEAMS

Difficulties found with teams in a work environment include:

- Lack of alignment on a vision
- Unclear team objectives and outcomes
- Unclear team boundaries (area of responsibility or frame of reference)
- Unclear team membership
- Divided loyalties by members among a number of teams
- Lack of group participation and facilitation skills
- Lack of team distinctions
- Lack of processes to resolve conflicts
- Lack of meeting and consensus decision-making skills
- Insufficient resources and back-up systems
- Creating a team unnecessarily when one person can do the job
- Not having decision-making autonomy
- Not having a coach

TEAM TRAINING

Organizations shifting from hierarchical to team-based structures often presume that people know how to be effective in teams without training. This is a big mistake. Working effectively in teams is an enormous shift for people used to reporting individually to a manager. Training to work effectively in groups and to facilitate groups is a necessary part of this training. It is unfair to throw people into teams, leave them to figure it out, then disband the teams when they don't work effectively. That is like trying to create a professional sports team from people who don't know the rules of the game and have no coach.

Coaching

In this chapter the role of the coach and the person being coached—the "coach-ee"—is explored. At the end of the chapter we provide a section on buddy relationships.

THE COACHING RELATIONSHIP

The coaching relationship is a useful and powerful one when you are ready for a challenge. It is powerful to have another person help you become the best you can be. All great athletes and sports teams have coaches. Coaches commonly assist in attaining physical fitness and are becoming more common as advisers to managers and other business people. Coaching can work for just about any project.

Coaching is a contracted relationship between two people, or one person and a group or team. Usually there is one coach and one or more people being coached. Coaching is a set of skills, some of which are generic (common to all situations) and some of which are specific to a particular field.

Working with a coach to achieve an objective can be empowering. It can be a powerful partnership that enables us to do what might be impossible on our own. A coach is a rigorous ally who will not let us subvert ourselves from our goals. If it is freely chosen and not imposed, coaching is a peer relationship based on trust and commitment.

THE ROLES

Coaching requires two roles: coach and "coach-ee." Sometimes two people can alternate the two roles. A reciprocal arrangement can work well but requires maturity, clarity and a clear contract.

THE CONTRACT

Coaching is a relationship conducted by agreement. A coach cannot be imposed on someone. A coach is someone who is committed to helping the person being coached to meet certain objectives. A coach is usually involved in the objective-setting process. The contract is usually written down and may describe how each person will relate to the other. A sample contract appears on the next page. (See Process 52, *Setting up a coaching or mentoring contract*.)

CHOOSING A COACH

Coaching requires mutual respect and a willingness to be honest and rigorous. A coach needs to be able to see through the patterned behavior of the person being coached (those "stuck" and limiting ways of doing things), to identify what is missing and to say honestly what he or she sees. A coach needs to encourage and acknowledge the progress made. A coach must have time for coaching and be prepared to make it a priority. A coach needs to believe in the person being coached and in that person's ability to achieve his or her objectives. A coach often, but not always, needs to understand the technical requirements of a particular field.

BEING COACHED

Deciding to work with a coach can be a big step to take. It is easy to confuse coaching with teaching and advice-giving. You can take or leave advice, and you can either absorb, sleep through or rebel against teaching. The person who is coached must have a sense of trust in the coach and a willingness to surrender to coaching. The person being coached must be willing and able to try the coach's suggestions without resistance or argument. A resistant coach-ee is poor material for coaching.

Coaching is often difficult to accept because the coach will suggest you

Coaching Contract between Julie Strong and Anne Bailey

DATE:

PURPOSE:
For Julie to be in business as a consultant in three months' time.

SPECIFIC ACHIEVEMENTS:
Five contracts in place.
Business license obtained.
Office set up.
Staff employed.
A one-year strategic plan for company.

TIME-FRAMES:
Coaching contract until specific date in three months' time.
Contract to be reviewed on ___. Julie will review her achievements, how the contract has worked for her, and complete or re-negotiate her contract.

AGREEMENTS:
All content is confidential.
Start and finishing times will be respected.
A regular meeting of 1 hour at 8 a.m. every Tuesday at Anne's office.
Julie may choose to phone during office hours, 9 a.m. to 5 p.m., for any issue she wants to discuss that relates to her contract.
It's OK for Julie to let off steam, be annoyed, upset.
Its OK to make mistakes.
Keep going, even when it's hard.

FEES: (Add agreed fee here.)

do things differently. This can be confrontational. Your automatic reaction may be to resist, and to feel you are misunderstood or are not good enough. You have learned to do something one way over a long period of time. You may be attached to your behavior even if it does not always lead to the results you want. We usually don't enjoy being confronted or challenged. You may react by wanting to discount the coach-ing or blame the coach rather than trying something new. Or you may want to blame yourself for not being perfect already. Watch for these automatic reactions. Get past them to accept the coaching.

Give coaching a fair trial. After that, you will find it helpful to review its usefulness to you. If you often argue with your coach, carefully consider whether you are *able* to be coached. You may be caught in patterned behavior that gets in the way of your progress. If you consistently take your coach's suggestions, give them a fair try and still do not get results, you may want to reconsider the coaching contract.

BEING A COACH

Coaching requires commitment from both the person being coached and the coach. Both parties are committed to the coach-ee reaching the agreed objectives. The relationship will founder without this commitment. Maintaining the commitment is a big part of the coach's role. An effective coach will maintain commitment to the coach-ee's objectives even when that person's commitment waivers and she or he wants to give up. For coaching to work, a coach has to be more committed to the coach-ee than the coach-ee is to him- or herself.

To train yourself to coach others, it is important to have lots of experience in being coached yourself. You will have learned some of what works and what doesn't work. However, what worked for you may not be what works for someone else. Remember that people are motivated in different ways.

Telling someone what to do isn't usually the best way to coach. It is much more empowering **to provide access.** The following two questions are really useful: **What will provide access** for the person being coached to the distinctions they need to know about? **What will provide access** to the person being coached in discovering how to achieve his or her goal?

Providing proper access to information is the key difference between showing someone how to read a map and telling them how to get to a destination. We like to distinguish among three levels of learning: getting it, knowing you've got it and providing access to it for someone else. Each level requires a different level of understanding. Coaching is at the third level.

The basis of the coaching contract is the commitment the person being coached has made and the vision that led him or her to take on the present challenge. Always come back to this. This is what will motivate the person being coached. Ask the coach-ee to write, draw or cut out a picture that represents the realization of the project and have him or her post the representation of the goal in an obvious place.

Design a framework—an action plan—with the person being coached for the realization of the project. Set it up together and agree on the details. A conversation to set up an action plan might include the following questions:

What is something you can do to have _____ happen?

What resources do you have or need to do that?

Is there anything stopping you from having that happen?

Is there a small step you can take now toward completing the (large) project?

Can you draw up a plan that will get you from A to B?

What support will you need to implement the plan?

Make sure the steps are realistic and the coach-ee is committed to them. Have the person you are coaching write down the details, and be sure each of you keeps a copy of it. Post the written statement somewhere obvious so the coach-ee and the coach can see it every day.

Agree on your contract—how you will work together. Ask the coach-ee what works for him or her and take note. We mostly know how we are best supported. Some people respond to a gentle nudge; others like a rigorous coaching relationship. Usually it works best for the coach-ee to take as much initiative as possible; for example, being the one to call the coach at an agreed time. Decide how often you will meet or talk over the phone. It works best to have regular check-in points.

When coach-ees are struggling or off track, usually they will stop communicating with you. This is frequently the first thing that happens. "I forgot to phone" is a huge alarm bell. Don't wait more than an hour after the agreed-upon time to act. Contact the coach-ee. Something is usually happening and the coach-ee is using it to disempower him- or herself. Find out what disempowering messages the coach-ee is sending himself and try to disarm or interrupt them. The conversation might go something like this:

"Hi, Bill, I didn't get your phone call. What happened?"

"I forgot. I got tied up with Henry and the time escaped me."

"How is your project going? You were going to do X and Y."

"Well, actually I had trouble getting X done because Z happened."

"What else happened?"

"Well, actually I'm not sure I want to do X any more. Perhaps it isn't the way to proceed."

"How do you feel about doing it?"

"Actually I feel scared."

"Yes, it is scary. You are a brave person for taking that on. Remember, you decided it was a good idea because ____."

"That's right. I'd forgotten that. I'll do it tonight."

"OK. Phone me when you have done it tonight."

"OK, bye."

Remember, you are always there to support the coach-ee. Don't get into your own stuff and start making judgments about them or their actions. We are all forgetful or lazy or scared at times. That is why we need a coach. The mind works in a million different ways to disempower us and rob us of victory in our projects. An effective coach is a master at outwitting disempowering conversations. (See Process 53, *Coaching—skills and insights*.)

WHAT TO WATCH OUT FOR

Both coach and coach-ee need to be aware that they can transfer inappropriate roles and emotions to each other. For example, the coach might transfer her unfulfilled ambitions to the coach-ee, or the coach-ee could relate to the coach as a parent or fall in love with her. To some extent this transference is inevitable. It is a good idea to do an identity check periodically. (See Process 35, *Identity check*.)

BUDDIES

A buddy is a friend at work (or anywhere else, really). It can be fun to use a buddy system at work for new staff and for learning new tasks. It is important for people to choose their own buddies because they need to share experiences with one another and create rapport.

IN THE ORGANIZATION

Buddies can also be helpful for keeping communication open among people working in different parts of or with different functions in an organization. The buddy system is a way of making informal networks overt, and it is helpful whether the organization is large or small. People working on different projects can "buddy up" and keep one another informed. This keeps communication channels open throughout the organization. Nobody needs to feel left out; any one person can have several buddies. Buddies know it is OK to phone one another to catch up; in fact, it is expected to happen regularly.

Buddies look out for one another and notice if something is going wrong. They can offer help quickly and encourage their partner to talk things through. They can offer suggestions and coaching if there is agreement about this role.

One charitable organization we know of uses this system for communicating between the board and the staff. Each board member has a portfolio of responsibility, and has a staff buddy who works in that area. The staff member keeps the board member informed of what is happening, and the board member shares his thoughts in turn. This buddy system keeps the board members involved. They are better able to make suitable decisions when issues come before them. Staff members find they have less explaining to do to the board because the board member takes on this role for them, accurately.

OUTSIDE THE ORGANIZATION

A buddy outside an organization can also be a useful relationship, particularly if you are new either to the organization or to the function you fulfill within it. Neither a coach nor a mentor, a buddy is a friend— someone to rave to, to share with, to complain to; a listening ear. It can be useful to create this relationship consciously rather than use your friends for this purpose. Ask if it's OK to use part of your time together to let off steam about your work. Seek agreement rather than doing it and hoping your buddy won't be bored by it. Often we abuse our friends by being unconscious about how we interact with them—by not giving them any choices. Create the freedom for them to say, "That's enough for now."

Mentoring

Mentoring is a relationship based on trust, respect and a loving connection between two people—both parties give and receive. A mentoring relationship usually arises spontaneously and, like friendship, requires nurturing. A mentor is one of the most precious relationships we can have. To have several in one's lifetime is a wonderful gift. A mentor can make life a lot easier for a young person or someone entering a new area of work or life. For a mentor there is great satisfaction in contributing to the protégé's future.

A mentor has the skills, experience, understanding and networks the protégé values and wants. The protégé has skills, abilities and potential that are seen and valued by the mentor. The protégé seeks to learn from the mentor. The mentor seeks to pass on what he or she knows to someone who is receptive and appreciative. Often the mentor is towards the end of a career or life stage and the protégé is at the beginning. The initiative for a mentoring relationship usually comes from the protégé.

The mentor shares experience and offers suggestions and advice. The mentor gives the protégé a helping hand, an easier route to gaining knowledge, experience and contacts. The mentor may also offer coaching. The protégé offers appreciation and a willingness to learn and develop.

A mentor is a teacher. However, only rarely is a mentor a formal teacher.

Mentoring is primarily a personal and informal relationship. Roles are clear and there is usually an age difference between the two people involved. The roles are not reciprocal, as they can sometimes be in coaching.

CHOOSING A MENTOR

Before choosing a mentor, consider whom you already know and admire in a field you have an interest in learning more about. Sometimes a mentor just needs recognition. They are already there, keeping a watchful and supportive eye on you. They can often see in you something of themselves in an early work or life stage. If there is someone already playing this role for you, you may want to recognize them. Let them know you see them in this light. This is a gift—to recognize and appreciate someone's support and affection for you. You may decide to meet on a more regular basis.

If no mentor is there, you may want to start looking for one. Look for someone you like, admire and respect. Cultivating a relationship with someone who can help you but whom you don't respect is unlikely to be healthy or nurturing.

Some agencies offer mentoring services. These are a little like a dating service. You may want to interview a number of people before you decide on a suitable relationship. It is important that you like and respect one another.

HOW TO BE AN EFFECTIVE MENTOR

Being a mentor is usually a great pleasure. It is the opportunity to pass on what you know to an appreciative person who is eager to learn. Encourage and support your protégé's professional growth and development. The point is not just to have someone listen to you, however; you need to listen, too. Listen for the potential of the person and the skills and experience they need to develop. Support them to move at a pace that works for them.

Avoid projecting your own unresolved ambitions on your protégé. Encourage him or her to develop a unique path. Be patient and show support when things don't go well. Let your protégé complain about things, but not too much. Encourage her or him to turn complaint into opportunity.

It helps to view the protégé as your equal—someone you respect, who has yet to reach his or her full potential. Avoid the parent-child relationship. Your role is to empower this person so she or he can be fully her- or himself. It is totally up to your protégé as to how far to develop at any time. One of the hardest things for mentors to see and accept is that their protégés may not want to develop all their potential. This decision must be respected.

It can be a hard lesson to see someone stopping themselves when you know they can do more. Remember, however, that the relationship is always more important than the result. Maintain the relationship, and the results will probably come in time. If they don't, you will still have a strong relationship.

It can deepen the relationship if you can do fun things with your protégé. Do you share any hobbies or leisure activities? You may enjoy meeting your protégé's family and friends. At all times, remember that your relationship is of a specific nature, different from other friends and from family. Respect the limits as well as the joys of this special relationship.

Do interrupt attempts by the protégé to put you on a pedestal. There is only one way off a pedestal, and it is always down! You can interrupt this pattern by sharing your humanity. Admit that you sometimes fail, too, and let your protégé see your vulnerability. Share how your difficult times and failures affected you. This will equalize the relationship and allow it to deepen. A powerful mentoring relationship between two real and vulnerable people is one of the special joys of life. Don't sell yourself short by withholding your authentic, vulnerable self.

If you have coaching skills, you may also coach your protégé. It is essential to clarify when you are coaching and to create a separate contract for this.

Setting limits

It is OK to set limits and boundaries around your availability as a mentor, such as when you are available to visit or speak on the phone, and when you are not. Be clear about your limits and insist they be respected. People are demanding sometimes. You may want to include these provisions in a contract. (See Process 52, *Setting up a coaching or mentoring contract.*)

How to be an effective protégé

A protégé receives a gift, and it takes practice to learn how to receive gifts with grace. It is important not to fall into the parent-child mode if you are of that age difference. Watch for projections of this kind and seek to work this through using peer counseling techniques (*not* with the mentor). The mentor-protégé relationship is quite different from the parent-child relationship. The mentor-protégé relationship exists between two whole and equal people who have different levels of skill and experience.

Avoid putting the mentor on a pedestal. Someone on a pedestal can only fall off, and this could damage your relationship. Everyone is perfectly imperfect and human, which is another way of saying we all have faults.

Always retain responsibility for yourself. Don't give this away to anyone, no matter how much you admire them. You are responsible for your own life and actions and must be accountable for your own choices. Ask for and receive advice, suggestions and coaching, but always remain your own person. Don't do anything just because someone else suggested it. You must make your own choices. It is OK to not take advice. Explain to your mentor why you decided against his or her advice.

Remember to appreciate your mentor. Thank them for their help. A card or small gift can mean a lot. Remember their birthday. Get to know them on a personal level.

Setting limits

You may need to set limits, especially if your mentor gets over-enthusiastic or has a strong personality. It is OK not to accept advice or suggestions but, if you find yourself doing this a lot, you may not have the right mentor. It is OK to set boundaries and limits. This is true for both parties, and is a good thing to discuss and agree on. Your boundaries may be quite different. That's normal. The boundaries of both parties need to be respected.

THE CONTRACT

A mentor-protégé relationship is mostly informal. It is helpful to recognize and talk about the relationship, though, and discuss both people's expectations as freely as possible. The frequency of meetings, availability, hopes and fears need to be discussed. If coaching or other techniques are to be used they need to be contracted.

If the relationship is formed through an agency, there may be restrictions on the number of meetings. There may be a cost involved.

It's a good idea to review the mentoring arrangement from time to time, perhaps every three months if it is ongoing. Set aside a time to review, and use a process such as sharing what's on your mind as well as reviewing your contract if you have one. If the relationship was developed through an agency, a formal review mechanism may come into play after a number of contacts.

TOOLS OF MENTORING

The kinds of tools you might use as a mentor include:

- Listening
- Talking through ideas
- Sharing experiences
- Introducing your protégé to interesting or helpful contacts
- Sharing information
- Recommending books and training programs
- Brainstorming
- Coaching
- Facilitating processes
- Giving advice (sparingly)

- Giving feedback
- Introducing to networks
- Being together in silence

WHAT TO AVOID

For a mentor, it is good to avoid:

- Referring a lot to the distant past
- Giving lots of advice
- Being patronizing
- Probing into the protégé's personal life
- Talking a lot about yourself
- Transference of roles and emotions

For a protégé, it is good to avoid:

- Knowing everything already
- Telling the mentor "how it is now"

Both need to avoid:

- Sexual involvement
- Transference of roles and emotions

(See also chapter 10, *Coaching*, "What to watch out for," page 95.)

Peer counseling

C
H
A
P
T
E
R

12

This chapter suggests that workplaces are often repressive, introduces the theory of peer counseling, and suggests how this method can be helpful in the context of peer relationships and co-operacy.

REPRESSIVE CULTURES

Our dominant Western culture is dependent on concepts of science and rationality. It tends to be emotionally, psychically, intuitively and spiritually repressive.

Repressive practices have been passed down from one generation to the next for hundreds of years. Education, parenting practices and social norms carry strong messages about emotions, psychic abilities and spiritual experiences—whether they are acceptable and in what form. We call this *socialization*.

The workplace tends to value rational thought above all else. Intuition, hunches, emotions and spirituality are seen as unreliable and irrational. It is not understood or valued that these capacities are in a different domain of knowing and vitally contribute to our ability to be sensitive to ourselves and our needs, to others and their needs, and to the world and its needs. The inability to claim all our capacities means we become alienated from parts of ourselves. We are out of touch with parts of our wholeness. (See Process 55, *Emotional conditioning*.)

EMOTIONAL COMPETENCE

Expressing emotions in the workplace is often regarded as a sign of weakness. Women who cry at work are likely to be considered unsuitable management material. Men who fail to "control" their anger will not get to be top managers. If they express fear or grief they may be referred to as sissies, meaning "woman-like," weak and irrational.

Repressing emotions all the time can lead to emotional and physical illness. It also affects our ability to be with others when they are expressing their emotions. We may either find our own emotions triggered inappropriately, or find it hard to be with the person in an empathetic way.

This does not mean that all emotional expressions are OK in the workplace. It is important to make a distinction between expressing emotions safely and appropriately where they relate to what is happening in the moment or in context, and expressing distress from the past that is triggered by something in the present situation. Unfortunately, very few of us can make this distinction or, if we do, have sufficient skill to separate the two.

We have a pressing need for education that enables us to access our emotions and emotional triggers and to express them in safe ways. Through expressing our emotions appropriately we learn that we are all vulnerable in some way. And by recognizing this on a deep, experiential level, we become more human and more able to live, work, cooperate with and heal ourselves and others.

The ability to understand and work with our emotions safely is called *emotional competence*, which involves:

- Being able to identify, own and accept all emotions in ourselves

- Understanding that the expression of grief, fear and anger can be healing, rather than "breaking down" or "losing control"

- Being able to express our emotions either now or later as a choice, and having a range of options for doing so, including peer counseling and therapy

- Understanding childhood trauma and its effects in adult life, and recognizing the hurt child within each of us

- Recognizing when we have been triggered by something from the past, rather than by the present situation

- Recognizing patterns or distress in ourselves and others, in organizations and in society

(See Process 56, *Emotional competence check.*)

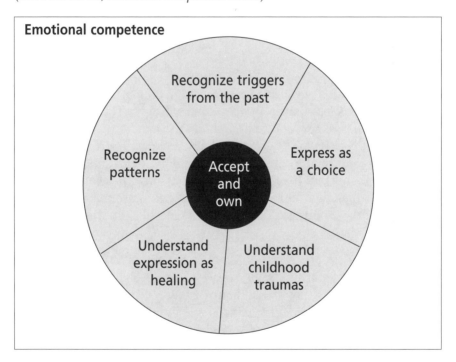

Emotional competence

Recognize triggers from the past

Express as a choice

Accept and own

Recognize patterns

Understand expression as healing

Understand childhood traumas

THE ROLE OF COUNSELING

Counseling is the generic word applied to educational or therapeutic work on oneself in the domain of the emotions or psyche. Most counseling takes place between a professional counselor and a client, who goes to the counselor for help in working through problems. The counselor is the expert; the client relies on the knowledge, experience and ethics of the counselor. The client goes through a process with the counselor. This can involve dependence on the counselor, at least for a while.

The counselor has knowledge and positional power. Counselors determine the methods and techniques used and may not explain these to the client. The counselor makes suggestions, which carry considerable weight. The session is held at the counselor's office (their territory).

The client shares his problems and vulnerability. The counselor does not share hers. After the counseling, the client may have a greater self-understanding for solving future problems, depending on the approach of the counselor.

PEER COUNSELING

Peer counseling is a very different way of working. The basis of this approach is to keep power in the client's hands. The client is self-generating, self-directing and self-monitoring.

A group of peers learns counseling skills and how to be a client in a safe environment, and then individuals contract with other, similarly trained peers to use these skills to work on their own issues. The client knows the techniques being used and is able to use them himself. The client can ignore any of the "counselor's" suggestions whenever he wants to.

CONTRACTING

Counseling sessions are reciprocal—that is, the pair alternates the roles of client and counselor in the same session. They usually contract for the same amount of time, say half an hour each way. The client instructs the counselor as to the desired intervention level and the particular techniques they would like used. The sessions are client-directed.

The client chooses the issue and the approach to it. The counselor does not give advice or interpretation. The counselor helps the client uncover thought and behavior patterns that are limiting or confusing the client, and enable the client to release pent-up distress (catharsis).

In any session both parties share their vulnerabilities and have equal time. They choose any venue they like and have the same skills.

PEER-COUNSELING NETWORKS

The peer-counseling model is used in the United States, the United Kingdom, Europe and New Zealand under the names *co-counseling* and *re-evaluation counseling*. A number of networks of peer counselors exist in different countries and through international contacts found on the Internet. Training is available through the networks. At Zenergy, we are happy to put you in touch with these networks (see page 256).

THEORY OF CO-COUNSELING

The theory and practice of co-counseling was created by Harvey Jackins in 1965 in what is known as *re-evaluation counseling*, and was developed further by John Heron as *co-counseling* in 1977. Here is a summary of the theory's main ideas:

Emotions occur as the result of basic personal needs being met or unmet. These basic needs are: to love and be loved, to understand and be understood, and to choose and be chosen. When love needs are met, the emotion is delight and joy. When love needs are not met, the emotion is grief and sorrow. When understanding needs are met, the corresponding emotion is interest, curiosity and fascination. When understanding needs are not met, the emotion aroused is fear and confusion. The emotion associated with being given choice is enthusiasm and zest. When choice is denied, the response is frustration and anger.

Needs that are not met lead to emotional pain and distress. We all have distress because it is not possible to go through life and have all needs met. The expression of distress through its related emotional expression is the natural form of healing emotional pain. If the distress is not expressed, it becomes repressed, stored in the body and displaced into other behavior. Displaced behavior, if not interrupted, becomes patterned and repetitive.

For example, if a child is not allowed to express her emotions she will act them out in some other way. A child who is not allowed to express her grief and anger at the arrival of a sibling may turn this into jealousy and hatred of the new baby. In an adult, pent-up anger may be expressed inappropriately over a small incident such as discourtesy by a driver in another car. This person may tailgate the other car or hit the other driver in an inappropriate expression of pent-up rage. (See Process 54, *Parental messages*.)

The four major ways of working in co-counseling are: regression and catharsis, celebration and affirmation, action planning and transpersonal expression.

CATHARSIS AND REGRESSION
Catharsis is a way of breaking up patterned behavior and releasing the emotional pain at its core. Grief is released by tears and sobbing, anger by yelling and movement, fear by trembling and shaking. As well as the healing that results from the release of locked-up emotions, spontaneous insights follow in their wake. These insights allow a valid part of the person to be reclaimed and integrated. Regression is a technique used to go back in time to an incident, often in childhood, that was a source of repressed pain.

CELEBRATION
This involves techniques to practice celebration, affirmation and unconditional regard of self, others and the world.

ACTION PLANNING
Releasing past hurts lets people create new futures for themselves. They can pay attention to different ways of planning for the future, including methods for overcoming blocks that could get in the way. These plans may be personal, social or political.

TRANSPERSONAL EXPRESSION
The transpersonal relates to spiritual needs and expression, and includes exploring and tapping into one's connection and relationship to divine life—being part of a greater whole, and attending to the life of the spirit, feeling resonance with the divine Other.

Map of basic emotional needs

RESULT	Acceptance of self and others ↑	Make sense of the world ↑	Perform and achieve ↑
RESPONSE WHEN NEEDS ARE MET	Joy and delight ↑	Curiosity, interest, adventurousness ↑	Enthusiasm and zest ↑
BASIC EMOTIONAL NEEDS	To love and be loved ↓	To understand and be understood ↓	To choose and be chosen ↓
RESPONSE WHEN NEEDS ARE UNMET	Grief and sorrow	Fear and confusion	Anger and frustration

REPRESSIVE CULTURE Don't cry; don't be frightened; don't show rage.

Distress. Denial of emotional pain. Distorted distress acted out as patterned behavior.

NATURAL HEALING	Sob and cry ↓	Tremble and shake ↓	Rage and storm ↓
RESULT	Acceptance of self and others	Make sense of the world	Perform and achieve

Adapted from John Heron's *Feeling and Personhood*.

TRAINING

Training as a co-counselor involves 40 hours of group training. After this, the participant can join a network of co-counselors. Weekly or bi-monthly sessions can then be contracted with other co-counselors in the network. Sessions can last half an hour or more, depending on what you prefer. Advanced training is also available in many countries.

COMMUNITY BUILDING

Co-counseling also encourages setting up networks and doing community-building work of various kinds, including living, working and skills exchanges. The hope is that people will relate to each other and the wider society in new ways through the widespread use of these skills.

Peer-development groups

We define a *peer group* as *a group of two or more people engaged together in a self-selected purposeful activity, with clear membership and a recognition of equal worth as persons.* There are many different kinds of peer groups—sporting, play, hobby, work, learning, development, spiritual and more. *Peer-development groups* is the over-all term we use for groups commonly known as *personal-development groups, peer-support groups, support groups, peer supervision groups, men's groups, women's groups* and so on.

In this chapter we look at peer-development groups with a focus on personal and work/professional development. The most useful groups we have been part of tend to adopt a whole-person, inclusive approach, with participants freely choosing their own personal/work limits in line with the group purpose and contract.

Peer-development groups are a powerful tool for individual and group learning. They involve:

- Building a high level of trust and honesty

- Use or development of the ability to reflect upon and recognize one's own learning and areas of growth

- Development of highly tuned listening skills, and the skills to give clear and constructive feedback

- Exercise of both compassion and rigor
- Honoring individual autonomy above group agreement
- Understanding the dangers of group-think and scape-goating, and avoiding these traps
- Group members learning to recognize their own and others' patterned-behavior thinking and how to interrupt it sensitively

Skills for effective participation in peer-development groups are a growing body of knowledge. There may be training courses in your community or area. Our company, Zenergy, offers a variety of training programs in this area, including group participation and facilitation skills. Our two other books, *The Zen of Groups* and *The Art of Facilitation*, deal with these topics also.

SETTING UP A PEER-DEVELOPMENT GROUP

Initiating a peer-development group involves: clarifying the purpose of the group to the extent that you can tell it to others; identifying people with whom you would like to form a group; and inviting them to join you. You may want to call it *a support group, an enrichment group, an empowerment group* or *a development group*. Use whatever name works for you.

PURPOSE

The purpose of such a group is best described in terms of specific focus. For example:

- Starting out in a job
- Being supported as a woman/man in the world
- Going into business as an independent practitioner/contractor
- Setting up an organization or company
- Taking on responsibility for leading projects
- Becoming a new parent
- Coping with teenagers

- Overcoming addiction
- Becoming a teenager
- Coping with parents
- Approaching 40, or another age
- Getting fit
- Studying after a break
- Studying a particular topic
- Renovating the house
- Living with roommates
- Saving to travel
- Supporting one another's projects
- Living magnificently
- Finding a job after losing one through a merger

CHOOSING GROUP MEMBERS

Someone will need to take the initiative to set up the group. This will need to be you! Think about the people you know and admire, the people you would really like to be in a group with—the ones you may be nervous about asking. Ask them—chances are they feel the same. Think about whether a variety of skills and experience will be useful. This will depend on your purpose. Do you want a mix of men and women? Be careful about hidden agendas. Don't set up a support group to get to know someone to whom you are sexually attracted. That won't work.

Discuss the composition of the group with the prospective members and reach a consensus before you meet. You all need to be compatible. It is hard to ask someone to leave the group if it is not working out. Choose people who are able to make and stick to their commitments.

VALUES

You may also want to consider the values of other prospective group members. Are they similar to yours? Could differences lead to arguments rather than support? What key values do you want to be shared? Setting a group culture is helpful to bring values into behavior. A group culture sets the stage for how you will work together. It addresses issues such as confidentiality, punctuality and commitment.

SIZE

The size of the group is important and will depend on what you want to accomplish in the group. If you want in-depth sharing and discussion of issues, it is best to keep the group small. Three to six people is a good number. If the group involves each person having equal time of, say, half an hour each, a four-person group will take 2-1/2 hours—half an hour each, plus time for greeting and leave-taking.

A six-person group can work well if it is facilitated by one member. Alternatively, you could rotate the role to monitor time-frames and intervene if people get off track. Larger groups can be effective, but they tend to require a facilitator or meeting leader, and not everyone will get to speak at any one meeting.

Our favorite number is three or four people, because that leaves plenty of time for in-depth sharing.

FREQUENCY OF MEETINGS

It also helps to clarify at the beginning the expected frequency of meeting and the number of meetings envisioned, and reach agreement on these. Some groups meet weekly, some biweekly or monthly. What might work for your group? The frequency will depend on the purpose of the group and the availability of members to meet.

WHERE AND WHEN TO MEET

Where will you get together? Some alternatives are:

- In one person's home
- In everyone's home on a rotating basis
- In a café or coffee shop
- In a private workplace area

Ensure that you are not interrupted by people and phones if your group involves in-depth sharing.

TIME

And what time of day will you meet—morning before work, noon, mid-afternoon, late afternoon? Any of these can work well, and so can other times. Set a time limit for your sessions—an end time. The length of time will depend on the number of people involved and the depth to which you wish to go. Two hours for four people is a guide. Shorter times (for example, one hour) can work if you are all very focused.

EXAMPLES

Dale belongs to two peer-development groups. One began as a group to support its four members who were setting up in business as self-employed people. Members engage in related areas of work: There is a business coach, a management consultant, a psychologist and a facilitator. As trust developed, the agenda expanded to include personal as well as work issues.

The group meets for a meal at each person's place in turn, followed by a two-hour session, half an hour for each person. The group has been meeting for six years and includes longer planning sessions of 24 hours once a year, when members stay somewhere together and each has a three-hour session to plan the year ahead in depth.

The other group Dale belongs to began after a communication course attended by all the participants. It meets twice a month for a one-hour breakfast in a café. The group's purpose is to coach one another to use the technology from the course. The group conducts short, focused sessions of

10 minutes for each person. Together for five years, this group began with seven members. In the last year two members have left the city and one has dropped out. Another member is overseas at the moment. All the group members have taken on big personal and work projects—five are involved in global projects.

Anne belongs to a development group that started with the focus of taking a quantum leap in either the members' personal or professional lives. Anne met with one other person for several weeks while they both looked for two more people to join the group. This group has been meeting for three years. They have explored different meeting times, and currently meet at one member's house monthly for a shared evening meal and catch-up, followed by a two-hour session. One person has moved out of town but checks in with the group when he visits the city. Each person has a very different work focus. One is an events manager, one is a health manager, one a facilitator and one a tourism marketer.

Until he left the area, Bill belonged to a men's group for four years. It began with nine members after all had attended a men's workshop. One member left after the first contracted period of six months and one drifted away in the last year. The group met twice a month at each other's homes from 7:30 to 10:00 p.m. They usually began with a short ritual followed by a brief check-in with each person speaking briefly in turn. This was followed by each having an in-depth sharing of where they were as men in the world—the focus of the group. This sharing was usually uninterrupted, but feedback was asked for quite often. The group also met for longer sessions—half a day, overnight—and supported Bill as his "best men" at his wedding.

THE FIRST SESSION

At the first session of your group, attend to:

1. Introductions—getting to know one another

2. Establishing your purpose in meeting

3. Setting a culture—how you want to work together

4. Setting a structure—how you will structure your meetings (for example, equal time for each member)

5. Contracting for an initial number of meetings—say, six—and then reviewing

6. Setting a place and time to meet

SUBSEQUENT SESSIONS

FOR INDIVIDUAL TURNS DURING A GROUP SESSION

When it is your turn in the group, you are in charge. Choose your issue, and decide what you want from the other group members. Then:

1. Describe your scenario to the group. For instance:
   - A problem with a project
   - A successful project
   - A risk you have taken or want to take
   - An ethical dilemma
   - An issue
   - A decision you are making
   - A problem
   - A concern
   - An incident
   - A conversation that went wrong
   - An upset
   - A challenge
   - A recurring pattern
   - A difficult relationship
   - Self-care needs
   - Something you are ashamed about
   - Something you wish you had/hadn't done

2. Request one or more of the following:
   - Feedback (positive and constructive criticism)
   - Acknowledgment only

- Close listening without comment
- Coaching
- A brainstorming session
- Others' experience in similar situations
- Speculation as to what they might do
- Suggestions for role-plays
- Role-play by other group members
- Role-play including yourself
- Feedback on patterned behavior
- Feedback on blocks
- Wild ideas and fantasies
- Professional opinion
- Hurrahs!
- Boos!
- Free response—anything goes

Stop and remind the group if they are not giving you what you asked for. Or you may want to ask for something else.

3. Sum up the learning. The person having a turn now completes his or her session. He or she:
   - Sums up what has been gained
   - Makes an action plan
   - Makes a promise
   - Requests a coach for a week
   - Acknowledges him- or herself
   - Requests applause and acclaim

4. At the end of your session, thank the group and give them some feedback—what was helpful and what was not. (See Processes 58, *Peer-development mode*, and 59, *Peer-development process—incident review*.)

PLANNING AND COMMITMENT
Plan your sessions well in advance and give them the highest priority. In

our groups, members have flown back from different parts of the country so that they would not miss a meeting. If everyone in the group treats it as very important it will be just that.

Group development model

A summary of M. Scott Peck's model of the four stages of community can be usefully applied to group development. This model is found in his book *The Different Drum*.

STAGE ONE: Pseudo-community. People meet and are very nice to each other, avoiding conflict.

STAGE TWO: Conflict and chaos. An essential stage of an effective group. Members begin to challenge one another. Individuals struggle to win and have their norm prevail.

STAGE THREE: Emptiness. This stage often requires members to give up something to enable the group to move on toward achieving its purpose. There may be an expectation of how the group should be. Some individuals may withhold their ideas or issues, and these are getting in the way of the group moving forward. Some group members begin to share their own distress, their doubts, fears and inadequacies. People begin to stop acting as if they have everything under control, and become more authentic with each other. The group chooses to embrace both the light and shadow sides of life.

STAGE FOUR: Authentic community. People begin to speak with vulnerability and authenticity. There will be sadness, joy and extraordinary individual healing. Community is born.

DEVELOPMENT OF THE GROUP

Peer relationships are the basis of authentic community—a communion of whole people. Many groups of people are working to create deeply satisfying relationships based on love, tolerance and common values.

The group will go through several stages in its development. Be prepared for these, especially the second one—conflict and chaos.

WHAT TO AVOID IN YOUR GROUP

The key things to watch out for and avoid are:

- Domination of the group by one or two people
- Advice that has not been requested
- Lack of commitment—arriving late or not showing up
- Safety issues, particularly confidentiality

RITUALS

You may start to develop rituals around your group. You may always share food, light a candle, have a beer—whatever makes the occasion special.

EVALUATION

After the first contract period—say, six sessions—evaluate the usefulness of the group. What works and what doesn't work for each of you? Be rigorous. You may want to write down one another's comments. Choose whether or not some or all want to continue and for what period. You may want to invite others to join if some do not re-commit.

Set an evaluation for the end of the next period or regularly every six months if the group is ongoing. If problems come up and they are not being addressed, hold a special session to discuss the problems. (See Process 23.)

INTENSIVES

You may want to have a longer, more intensive session occasionally, as Dale's group does once a year. Her group goes away together for 24 hours. Each person has a three-hour session in which to explore plans for the year in some detail, using the others as facilitators and resource people.

BARTER

As an extension of the group activities you may want to consider bartering services among yourselves. Keep records of who did what so that no one feels taken advantage of in this respect.

PARTIES

Take opportunities to celebrate together—Christmas parties, anniversary parties or other celebrations are great ways of acknowledging each other.

Peer reflection

The focus of this chapter is peer reflection—learning together through self-reflection and the reflection of others while or after we are involved in work. It is important to reflect on and learn from experience. After all, this is the capacity that makes us uniquely human. Traditional education from school, training programs and our own reading are all useful.

When we take on a project or task and achieve it in whole or in part, we learn along the way. We need ways of recognizing, capturing and integrating what we have learned so we can develop more fully and be more effective in the future. Individual reflection is useful, of course. Group reflection is powerful because we can reflect together, share insights and build on one another's insights. By learning together we can learn more than we could on our own.

In this chapter we outline a number of peer-reflection methods: peer feedback, self- and peer assessment and peer-performance review.

PLANNING

Learning after the event is not a substitute for good planning at the start. Good planning reflects our level of learning because it represents what we have already learned, integrated and are able to put into practice. Good planning also includes the criteria for success. How will we know if we have been successful? SMART (Specific, Measurable, Attainable, describing a Result and Time-bound) objectives and performance measures can help here.

We also need to be clear about our purpose and what we plan to achieve—the mountain we plan to climb and where the summit is. And we need to remember details, such as to bring the flag to plant on top and the camera to record the event. We will want to know and demonstrate whether we were able to reach our goal.

The plan will also include a system for monitoring our progress at prearranged points along the way. These will be the review, learning and adjustment/correction points. This system will help us minimize wasting time, energy and resources on our journey.

How will we know we have been successful?

These elements taken together are helpful to remember as the *planning, action, reflection cycle.*

Even if we adopt an organic approach to planning—looking out as we move forward for signs and indications as to where to go next, uncovering the future rather than following structured plans—we will still have a purpose in mind; perhaps enjoying the journey itself. We will be learning things that will help us on subsequent journeys and we will be learning other things, less related to the journey, too. This learning is important also.

At the end of the journey we will reflect in depth on the learning to get as much as possible from it. We will scrape the barrel for learning in all areas of our whole being.

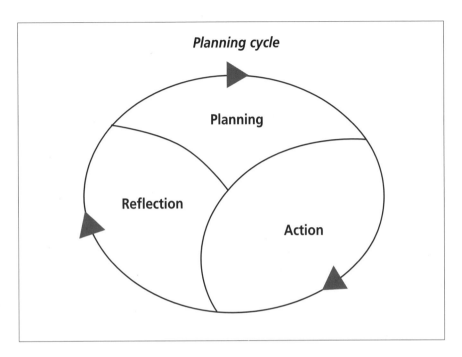

Planning cycle

Planning

Reflection

Action

FEEDBACK

One important tool for peer reflection is the giving and receiving of direct feedback. Direct, face-to-face feedback is a skill to be learned. It is also a gift. Because we tend to be our own severest critics, it can be a liberating experience to get direct feedback from co-workers. Direct feedback also interrupts cultural patterns of talking about others behind their backs and forces us to face up to what we are saying. It cuts out much of the back-stabbing from the workplace. It also allows for genuine acknowledgment to take place, something often missing from the workplace.

SUGGESTIONS FOR GIVING FEEDBACK

- Be specific.
- Be constructive.
- Avoid qualifying words, such as *very* and *almost*.

- Make eye contact.
- Speak to the person directly. Do not talk about him or her to others.
- Give criticism and acknowledgment equal weight.
- Be honest.
- Don't avoid.

(See Process 48, *Day-to-day feedback*.)

PROJECT FEEDBACK

At the end of a project, make time to get together with the other participants and reflect on what was learned. Ask yourself the following questions (or make up your own), and record the responses. Make sure everyone has a chance to respond to each question.

- What was the purpose of the project?
- What were the promised results (specific objectives and performance measures)?
- Were they stated clearly?
- To what extent were they achieved: all, some, a percentage?
- What other criteria were there for success?
- To what extent were they met: all, some, a percentage?
- What else happened?
- What was learned from the process?
  - Planning
  - Review points
  - Completion
- What "hiccups" in the process occurred?
- What disasters happened?
- What unexpected bonuses occurred?

- Did each individual contribute as planned?
- What did we learn that we are avoiding the mention of? Add this in.
- What do you know now that you did not know before?
- What will you do differently next time?

Here are three ways members of the group can share their answers to these questions.

PROCESS 1

STEP 1: Each person in turn reflects on the project, answering the questions they find relevant. They may include reflections on their own contribution. The others listen carefully and, at the end of the turn, a short question period is allowed for clarification only. Group members take turn keeping the notes about reflections made during this round.

STEP 2: Each person takes another turn, answering two more questions and recording the answers:

- What did you really learn?
- What did you learn that you will take with you to the next project?

PROCESS 2

STEP 1: Each person draws a picture that reflects his or her individual response to the project.

STEP 2: These drawings are shared with the group. Each person comments on his or her own drawing.

STEP 3: The group looks for patterns in the drawings. What do the patterns represent?

STEP 4: The group reflects on the patterns. What was learned?

VARIATION: Make a group drawing instead of, or in addition to, individual ones.

Process 3

STEP 1: Have a brainstorm session of what was learned from the project. You may want to break down the project into steps and have a brainstorm for each. Record ideas on a large white board.

STEP 2: Reflect on the comments. What were the themes? What were the key things learned? Highlight these.

STEP 3: Have each person write down what he or she learned individually, and what action he or she will take in the future.

VARIATION: Conduct the brainstorm as a team relay. Divide the group into two teams and ask each team to form a line at the back of the room, facing a white board that has been set up at the front. Armed with pens, team members at the head of each line run up to the white board and add a learning point to their team's column. Then they run back to the starting line and pass the pen to the next person in line. Continue until the white board is filled.

SELF- AND PEER FEEDBACK

Self- and peer feedback is reflection focusing on individual performance. The focus in this case is trained on the person more than on the project. Each individual assesses his or her own performance and then gets feedback from others.

SELF- AND PEER ASSESSMENT

Use the following informal group process for self- and peer assessment. This exercise is useful for individuals who want feedback for their own education as opposed to a formal performance review. It can be used as a means of reviewing individual performance or progress made in training.

STEP 1: Individual(s) who want feedback develop criteria for what they want feedback about. These could include:

- Skill level
- Contribution to others or project

- Willingness to accept challenge/coaching from others
- Self-care
- Time management
- Use of resources
- Presence
- Ability to engage others
- Ability to motivate others
- "Intentionality"—ability to stick to the purpose of the project through completion
- Starting and finishing
- Planning

Keep the criteria simple and concise—no more than five or six key areas.

STEP 2: A group meeting is set up and peers are invited as desired by the person receiving the feedback. The criteria are shared with the other group members. Provide written copies or write up on a sheet. Group members do not have to agree in their comments. Arrange for someone to record the comments if desired.

Note: The person receiving the feedback is in charge of this process. It is important to remain emotionally detached from the feedback, which will include nonrelevant comments and projections. Let feedback that is not helpful float past.

STEP 3: The person gives feedback to him- or herself against his or her own criteria: what was done well and what might be improved on next time. Other group members can pose questions for clarification only at the end.

STEP 4: The person advises the group of how he or she would like the feedback to be given: constructive criticism, then acknowledgment, and so on.

STEP 5: Each group member gives feedback in turn, addressing the same criteria—what the person did well and what could be improved.

STEP 6: The person receiving the feedback reflects on the feedback given and notes what was learned from it.

VARIATIONS:

- Positive feedback only
- One positive statement and one constructive criticism only
- Self-reflection only, without response

SELF- AND PEER-PERFORMANCE REVIEW

Peer-performance review is most effective when it fully honors the humanity of those involved. It can be an affirming and joyful experience of being fully acknowledged. This is best illustrated by processes that involve a high-trust group experience in which feedback is made openly and honestly. At best, this process is facilitated.

BACKGROUND

A number of formal methods of performance review are based on peer models. These include verbal and/or written evaluations of one another's work. In a hierarchical organization, one method is called *360° evaluation*, with people above, alongside and below in the hierarchy contributing. At present, much learning is taking place as to the most effective ways of creating peer processes for performance review in the workplace. Many people have had disappointing experiences from poorly planned or implemented processes.

INTRODUCING PEER-PERFORMANCE REVIEW INTO AN ORGANIZATION

Introducing peer-performance review into an organization requires education and careful negotiation. The process can enable and affirm those involved. However, it may be viewed with suspicion by people who are not familiar with the method. This will very likely be the case if the organization is hierarchical, and people are concerned about the unequal distribution of power. First introduce informal self- and peer-assessment practices so everyone can get used to the processes involved. This requires agreement by all concerned. An enabling method that is nonetheless introduced in a coercive way damages trust. You may need to hire a facilitator if these skills are not available within your organization.

CRITERIA

The key to effective peer-performance review is the development and agreement of the criteria against which each person is to be reviewed. These criteria must be developed at the time of performance planning—the beginning of the planning year or the project. The criteria need to be clear, concise and as objective as possible, and preferably quantifiable. If qualitative, they need to be based on recognized competencies. The criteria are negotiated and agreed to by the parties involved.

> **The secret of effective criteria is to**
> **have no secrets or hidden criteria.**

PEER-PERFORMANCE REVIEW PROCESS

STEP 1: At the beginning of the project or work period, develop criteria for the review. Negotiate and get agreement from all key people. It is preferable to work together as a group to develop these criteria. It works best if the first draft of the criteria comes from the person(s) being reviewed. The criteria are best kept clear and concise, with five or six key areas only.

STEP 2: At the end of the project or work period, arrange a time for the review. Choose a quiet, private, comfortable space where everyone can sit down and see one another. Allow two hours per person being reviewed. Make sure all the key people are present, keeping in mind that more than six people can appear rather daunting to the person being reviewed.

STEP 3: The person being reviewed prepares and writes down his or her own comments, and these become part of the review record. This person may want to practice presenting the review to a colleague beforehand. Each peer will also spend time reflecting on and considering the comments they would like to include. It helps to write these down. Choose a facilitator and recorder for the review process.

STEP 4: THE REVIEW MEETING

The facilitator or the person being reviewed introduces the process steps for the meeting. The time allowed for each step is negotiated—for example, introduction, 10 minutes; Phase 1, 30 minutes; Phase 2, 30 minutes (or 10 minutes for each peer); Phase 3, 10 minutes plus break time. Phase 4, 10 minutes.

Phase 1: The person being reviewed gives his or her own assessment of recent performance without interruption. Time is allowed for clarification questions at the end.

Phase 2: Each peer comments in turn. At the end of each turn the reviewer may ask clarification questions. As well as their own reflections, the peers comment on anything they noticed the reviewer over- or underestimated or left out. Record comments.

Phase 3: The person being reviewed pauses to think about the feedback, requesting a short break if necessary.

Phase 4: The person being reviewed reflects on the feedback that was shared and what he or she has learned from it. This is expressed verbally to the peers. Record these comments. The facilitator encourages the person being reviewed to end with self-acknowledgment. The facilitator thanks everyone for their contributions and for listening.

STEP 5: The person being reviewed reflects privately and considers what further training may be needed and also how differently he or she will plan and implement work in the next project or work period. It is helpful to discuss this with a colleague to ensure that the insight does not get lost. The colleague could be asked to act as a coach to help put what was learned in place.

Peer inquiry

The previous chapter focused on peer reflection and the powerful learning available from this technique. We could say that peer reflection is about teasing out what we *already know*. This chapter relates to learning also, but this time the focus is on how we think, what we *don't yet know* and what we don't *know* we don't know. It is the area of *inquiry* or *action research.*

Peer-inquiry methods recognize the power of inquiring with others, the enlarging and synergistic effect of sharing and building on one another's thinking. Inquiring together allows the development of group intelligence, which can potentially be much greater than that of an individual.

The key tool for inquiry is strategic questioning: *What about . . . ? What if . . . ? Imagine . . . !* It is about pushing the boundaries, exploring, innovating, going to new places. It is about human curiosity; a search for new ideas, new ways of thinking and doing things. Strategic questioning is a powerful tool for entering and working the new, co-operative–inclusive way. The skill lies in developing the most useful question.

To provide an opening into this area of inquiry, we will describe two methods: strategic dialog and co-operative inquiry. Both methods have been written about eloquently and in depth by others. Our purpose here is to introduce them to you. You may then want to read about them in more depth.

INQUIRY IS NOT DISCUSSION

Discussion is the usual way we interact with one another. One person talks, another adds something, perhaps triggered by the same or an associated idea, the first person agrees, disagrees, adds an opinion, interpretation, and so on. This is our normal mode of conversation.

In a group of people, the interaction becomes more complex. We jump in to the fray, adding our views, cutting in . . . sometimes everyone talks at once. Our discussions can be percussive and competitive. We seek to debate, score points off one another, win the argument.

This is the kind of discussion we have at parties, in cafés, at dinner, at home and at work. We often end up talking past one another and not feeling heard. It can be dissatisfying and bruising to relate to others in this way all the time. Here is a different way of conversing you might like to try.

STRATEGIC DIALOG

The word *dialog* comes from two Greek roots, *dia* and *logos,* which suggest the translation *meaning flowing through.* Dialog can be defined initially as a sustained, collective inquiry into the processes, assumptions and certainties that compose everyday experience.

Strategic dialog is a conversation that focuses on the whole and encourages participants to contribute the parts, the content. It is useful for complex issues where no one person has the answer. People weave a web of connections through their various contributions that enables new insights to emerge. Dialog seeks to uncover the beliefs and assumptions that lie underneath our thinking, and get to the heart of the matter.

Where does strategic dialog come from? The philosopher Martin Buber used the term *dialog* in 1914 to describe a mode of exchange among human beings in which there is a true turning to one another and a full appreciation of another person, not as an object in a social function, but as a genuine being. Patrick DeMaré and David Bohm developed this approach further in the 1980s.

DeMaré, a psychologist, proposed that large group "socio-therapy" meetings could enable people to engage in understanding and altering the cultural meanings in society, to heal the sources of mass conflict and violence or ethnic bigotry.

Bohm, a leading quantum theorist, saw dialog as a new way of paying attention—to perceive the assumptions taken for granted, the flow of the polarization of opinions, the rules for acceptable and unacceptable conversation and the methods for managing differences as they arose. The mindfulness embodied in dialog involves *awareness of the experience of thinking,* rather than reflection on it afterwards. The purpose of dialog is to create a setting in which conscious, collective mindfulness can be maintained. At that point, a group becomes open to the flow of a larger intelligence.

Strategic dialog is currently associated with the "learning organizations" work by Peter Senge, Juanita Brown and others. Part of their work has redefined organizations as communities of people who learn.

Bohm said three basic conditions are necessary for dialog: participants need to suspend their assumptions, holding them as if suspended before them; participants must regard each other as colleagues; and, there must be a facilitator to maintain the context of dialog.

To create a spirit of inquiry, it is helpful to:

- Choose a setting that minimizes normal distractions.
- Encourage informality, relaxation and personal relationships.
- Assure all voices are heard early on.
- Honor the knowledge that is alive and present.
- Focus on questions that create curiosity.
- Acknowledge that comfortable and uncomfortable reactions are normal.
- Demonstrate innovative and interesting tools, such as graphic facilitation.

To improve the quality of our thinking together, we can shift our awareness and notice:

- Not just the ideas themselves, but also the connections among them
- Not just conflicting views, but also differences bringing new insight to the whole
- Not just the topics discussed, but also the unspoken questions and issues arising from them
- Not just approval or disapproval, but also inner tension as clues to underlying assumptions
- Not just speaking and listening, but the significance of allowing silence

(Adapted from Juanita Brown and Sherrin Bennett in *Learning Organizations*.)

WHEN TO USE IT
Strategic dialog is useful for exploring interesting, difficult or complex issues for which there are no easy answers and in which participants have a strong interest. For example, a strategic dialog could explore the kind of organizations that might exist in the future.

SETTING THE ENVIRONMENT
The environment needs to be comfortable—sofas or comfortable chairs in a circle or, if a lot of people are involved, a number of small tables. The tables can be covered with paper and pens (provided to encourage people to doodle and draw as they talk and listen). If a large group of people is involved, the dialog will be directed by the facilitator, who will get people to move from table to table from time to time to share ideas. Some conversations will be held in small groups and some in the large group.

RECORDING
A great way of recording strategic dialog is through graphic facilitation. The person recording (the *recorder*) uses symbols and words to capture the flow of the conversation. This can be done on big sheets of paper or on an electronic white board. Symbols inspire the imagination and help access the right as well as the left side of the brain.

In a strategic dialog, the facilitator introduces a topic or issue and asks a question to begin the inquiry. This "strategic question" is designed to encourage participants to explore their own thinking. People respond in their own way and are willing to be fully involved without knowing where the conversation will lead. Participants listen to all the contributions as part of the whole. They listen not for what is right or wrong, but to get the value of each contribution and recognize the way in which it enhances the whole and furthers the conversation. It is the process of thinking together.

The role of the facilitator is to hold the question and bring people back to it, repeating the question when it begins to become submerged under other topics.

As the conversation unfolds, a new question will arise, either spoken by a participant or noticed by the facilitator, who listens for what is unspoken. This will enable the inquiry to go to a deeper level. The new question is then posed by the facilitator. This new question will uncover some of the assumptions and beliefs that underpin the conversation.

The conversation continues and a spirit of openness develops. Conversation begins to flow. The group is thinking together as one mind, and the shared meaning begins to emerge. What is spoken is heard more deeply. There is a sense of both subtlety and fullness. The silences become longer.

Sharing silence with another creates a bond that cannot be compared to ordinary exchanges. It helps us know that each of us is essential—a vibrating essence. When we sit quietly together we can sense that vibration—we can feel it singing in ourselves. When we speak, when we act, when we offer each other food and water, we give form to the essential vibration within us. We become, in a sense, living words. Words in combination make complete, meaningful phrases. Through this collaboration, potentials can be realized. Worlds are created. In the language of life, we are words of power. When we support the silence in one another, we discover that we each have been given to be. The silence in each of us is the medium through which the words we are may be spoken, clearly and purely. In silence we are revealed. This is universal and very personal.

[Gunilla Norris, *Cultivating Mindfulness in Everyday Life.*]

Co-operative inquiry

Traditional research distinguishes between the researcher who initiates, designs and implements the research, and the research subjects who are observed, manipulated and recorded. Research subjects have no involvement in the research design and, in some cases, may not know they are being researched. Where they are willing subjects, they may not know the purpose of the research or the reasoning behind the methods used.

Co-operative inquiry is a type of research in which the researchers also become the researched. All the people who design and develop the research are also fully involved as the only subjects of the research. The design is collective and the people involved are likely to have a large degree of autonomy in the way they involve themselves and the techniques they use individually as part of the research. Co-operative inquiry is an advanced form of action research.

Methodology

The methodology used in co-operative inquiry draws on aspects of the whole person, including the use of intuitive, emotional, spiritual and imaginative aspects, as well as conceptual ones.

Co-operative inquiry can be described as having a basic cycle with four phases that move from reflection to action and back to reflection again.

Phase 1—Formulation: A group of co-researchers agrees on the area of inquiry and identifies some initial propositions to explore. They may choose to explore some aspect of their experience, agree to try out in practice particular skills, or they may seek to change some aspect of their world. They also agree on a process by which they will record their own and each other's experience. They may agree on a recording method that involves a wide range of media, from observation notes, free-flow reflection, poetry, drawing, music, movement—individually, in twos, threes, sub-groups or the whole group. Variety contributes to a rich inquiry.

Phase 2—PRACTICE: The group applies the ideas and propositions in their everyday life and work. They observe and record the outcomes of their own and others' behavior. They observe the obvious and the subtle and look to see in what ways their original ideas do and do not accord with experience.

Phase 3—IMMERSION: The co-researchers become fully immersed in the activity and experience. They respond with any or all of the range of feelings, from excited to bored, engaged to alienated. They may forget to record their findings and may stumble on unexpected insights. They may be able to set aside their previous belief systems to allow for new, experiential insights to emerge.

Phase 4—REVIEW AND PLANNING: After an agreed-on period in Phases 2 and 3, the co-researchers reassemble to share the experiential data from these phases and to consider their original ideas in light of it. Depending on what they find, they may develop or reframe these ideas, or reject them and pose new questions. They may choose, in planning the next cycle of action, to focus on the same or on different aspects of the overall inquiry. The group may also choose to amend or develop its inquiry procedures—forms of action, ways of gathering data—in light of the experience.

REPEAT CYCLES

The four-phase cycle is repeated several times. Ideas and discoveries tentatively reached in early phases can be checked and developed; investigation of one aspect of the inquiry can be related to the exploration of other parts; new skills can be acquired and monitored. At the final meeting, for reflection, the research findings will be brought together and may be made available to others in some kind of written report and/or in some other kind of presentation.

VALIDITY IN CO-OPERATIVE INQUIRY

Co-operative inquiry claims to be a valid approach to research involving people because it relies on a collaborative encounter with experience. The validity of this encounter with experience depends on the high-quality, critical, self-aware, discriminating and informed judgments of the co-researchers—a method known as *critical subjectivity.*

The method is subject to all the ways that human beings fool themselves and each other in their perceptions of the world, including cultural bias, character defense and political partisanship. In particular, unconscious projection and consensus collusion present problems. Cycling between action and reflection, exploring the authenticity of participation in the group and using self-development methods to look at unacknowledged anxiety are three ways to counteract these issues, but there are other ways also.

Two leaders in this field of inquiry are John Heron and Peter Reason. John Heron wrote an excellent book on this subject, *Co-operative Inquiry.*

ZENERGY CO-OPERATIVE INQUIRY

From August to November, 1994, two of us, Dale Hunter and Anne Bailey, took part with two others, David Duignan and Peta Joyce (facilitator) in a co-operative inquiry: "How are we creating Zenergy's vision for co-operacy?" The rationale for the inquiry was to examine our own congruence in living out our vision. Excerpts from the summary we prepared at the end of the inquiry are below, to give you a sense of what took place:

WE ADDRESSED OUR ORIGINAL QUESTION BY DEVELOPING THE INQUIRY AND GENERATING FURTHER QUESTIONS AS FOLLOWS:

- What is co-operacy? When is it present/absent?
- Do we see co-operacy as present in our relationships?
- What is the strategic plan for co-operacy?
- What is missing/needs to be added?
- How do we implement the strategic plan? What would make it easier?
- What impact is Zenergy having on co-operacy in the world?
- What are the values and distinctions of co-operacy?
- What has become conscious or moved?

- What is distinguished in the world?
- What actions took place as a result?
- What did we learn that can be passed on?
- What is the relationship between co-operacy and the Zenergy community?

HOW RIGOROUS WERE WE?

- Nineteen out of 21 planned meetings were held.
- Individual self-assessment of commitments made and kept between meetings were: Anne, 50%; Peta, 85%; David, 45%; Dale, 60%; group aggregate, 60%.

WHAT HAS HAPPENED THAT WOULDN'T HAVE HAPPENED ANYWAY?

- Transformations of being
- Quicker group process
- Group alignment on the distinctions of co-operacy

WHAT DIFFERENCE WILL THIS MAKE IN THE WORLD?

- Developing the distinctions around a new word that will transform the future of the world

THE FOLLOWING DISTINCTIONS OF CO-OPERACY WERE DEVELOPED:

- Co-operacy is a way of being that honors our "connectedness" and uniqueness as whole people (inner and outer worlds, shadow and cosmic, joy and pain) in a whole universe.
- Co-operacy is action out of a concern for the highest good of all life.
- Co-operacy is generated through aligned intention, action and a willingness to cut through the junk.
- The value is in the process of consciousness, of co-operacy, of ourselves and each other, of other realms.
- Co-operacy is about allowing the oneness and "connectedness" of all things.

- Co-operacy is the natural state of being.
- Co-operacy is discovering what it is that blocks that state of being —fear creates the other imposed states on top of the natural order that is co-operacy.
- Co-operacy is a universal culture.
- Co-operacy encompasses the highest interests and well-being of all.
- Co-operacy is living from the heart.
- Co-operacy is a dynamic relationship among vision, strategic plan and us.
- Co-operacy is freedom from expected outcomes.
- Co-operacy is a release of energy.
- Co-operacy is intentionality (see page 82) without attachment to a particular outcome.
- Co-operacy is working with a common purpose.
- Co-operacy gives rise to action.
- Co-operacy arises out of being aligned with a purpose bigger than the people or organizations involved.
- Co-operacy occurs in the interaction of being human. It's like making music together—each instrument can be doing its own thing but somewhere there is a focus or harmony with others to bring it all together.
- Co-operacy calls us to be fully functioning beings—individually, organizationally and globally.
- Co-operacy is present when interactions empower all parties.

VALUES
- Honoring the individual
- Inclusiveness
- Clarifying contributions
- Variety of ways of working
- Not personality driven

- Organic origination; changing; learning
- Accountability-driven—"being" our word
- Interpersonal skills and awareness
- Process and trusting the process
- Alignment rather than agreement
- Intentionality (see page 82)
- Commitment
- Context of higher purpose
- Consciousness

BLOCKS TO CO-OPERACY

- "Sitting on my stuff"
- My fear that I don't have the right to express my perceptions
- Not giving myself permission to think fully; getting diverted
- I need to believe I have equal space and take some action
- Not allowing my vulnerability

PATTERNED BEHAVIOR

- How we sabotage ourselves and what we are doing in unconscious patterned behavior
- Interlocking control patterns among people
- Not having a group commitment to interrupt patterns
- Doing without love, compassion and vigilance

WITHHOLDING

- Is about fear of consequences (old patterns)
- Occurs within a context of a purpose
- Stops me from being fully present and self-expressed
- Is a thought that has been given meaning
- Is a fact that would make a difference if spoken and would deepen the relatedness between people
- Means I feel unsafe to speak, a little like death
- Sharing involves a risk
- Communication needs to be from love

Peer organizations

How do peers work together in the larger groupings we know as organizations? In this chapter we explore management, ownership and peer organizations as communities based on chosen values.

MANAGEMENT

Since the industrial revolution, organizations have been based mainly on the military model of command and control. Only top management has access to sufficient information to make major decisions. Planning is carried out at the top and commands are passed down the line, from boss to manager to worker, and the worker's role is to carry out the assigned tasks. Failure to carry out a specific direction by a manager is grounds for dismissal.

Businesses now, in the post-industrial environment, can be very large and/or global in scope. As mentioned before, only half of the biggest 100 economies in the world today are countries. The rest are giant multi-national corporations.

Companies may have bases anywhere in the world, where material resources and workers are most readily available at the best price. These bases move around, sometimes with devastating effects on local economies. At the same time, computer technology can now provide information to most parts of the world almost instantly.

It has become impractical to keep decision-making in the hands of a few at the top of big corporations. They have no more relevant information than locally based managers, and they are not in touch with local conditions. For these reasons decentralized organizations made up of separate, self-managing business units, or separate interlocking companies, are becoming a common model.

You no longer have to be big to be global in the information age, however. The *Economist* in London has only 55 journalists, but covers the world in scope and readership. Many Internet-based companies can be very small but operate globally.

At the same time, decision-making is becoming more complex. A wide range of skills and expertise may be needed to make good decisions. A number of people may need to be involved, each with some of these skills and knowledge. The intelligence of a group is required for complex decision-making. Co-operative structures, such as teams, strategic alliances and partnerships, are becoming favored over hierarchies, not for philosophical reasons but for purely pragmatic ones.

EXAMPLES OF NEW STRUCTURES

New organizational structures are emerging. Examples of these include the matrix, the doughnut, the cloverleaf or shamrock, and team-based organizations.

In the **matrix** structure, workers report to a number of people, depending on the nature of the task. There are still hierarchical levels, but they are more fluid, and individuals work to achieve negotiated objectives and outputs.

A **doughnut** organization is divided into two circles: a core of necessary jobs and necessary people, surrounded by an open, flexible space that is filled with flexible workers and flexible supply contracts. (See Charles Handy, *The Empty Raincoat*.)

A **cloverleaf** organization divides workers into three categories. A core of essential workers is backed up by contractors (consultants and self-employed professionals) and a flexible labor force (part-time and casual workers) to meet the demands of the market.

In a **team-based** organization, most of the work and task-related decision-making is carried out by groups of people organized into teams. Managers are retained but there are fewer of them. Their role is to coordinate and set parameters for the teams and take responsibility for overall strategic planning. They may be organized into a coordinating team and draw their membership from the other teams. (See chapter 9.)

Ricardo Semler's Brazilian company, Semco, is one often-cited organization structure. He divided that company into just three levels. Directors became "counselors," senior managers became "partners," and everyone else, "associates." He describes the results of this restructuring in his book, *Maverick.*

Du Pont, a U.S. corporation, is another frequently referred-to example of a team-based organization. Du Pont's goal is to become a development organization in which every employee is a source of creativity, and in which all employees are self-organizing. (See Michael Ray and Alan Rinzler, *The New Paradigm in Business,* page 147.)

OWNERSHIP

So much for management. What about ownership? The basic issue remains: Who owns the organization? Who are the shareholders? Who gets the benefit from the success of the organization? Who takes the risks of its failure?

Most public companies are now owned by institutions—investment funds, pension funds, insurance companies. The individual shareholder is almost a thing of the past. The average share-holding by these big investors can be short; in Britain it is four years. These investors are not involved in the companies in any direct way. They are mainly interested in short-term profit. They have been likened to bettors shifting allegiance from racehorse to racehorse, depending on the latest racing sheet. Some management theorists are now questioning whether ownership as it is now practiced is healthy for business.

Charles Handy favors the idea of business as self-governing, membership organizations. He feels that co-operatives of the past have often confused the functions of ownership and management, and that these two functions are best kept distinct. Evidence is mixed on employee share-ownership schemes, which companies have adopted to give their workers a stake in the organization. Handy believes the key to success is a real sense of membership; to his mind, this is where the difference will come. New kinds of legal structures will be needed. However, laws tend to follow practice, not lead it.

PEER ORGANIZATIONS AS COMMUNITIES

And what is an organization anyway? Is it a thing, an object to be manipulated by the people who own it? Are the people in it units of labor and human resources? Or is it a community of people—a living system, a collective consciousness? How we view an organization determines how we interact with it or are part of it.

This discussion is the essence of peer organizations. If an organization is a community of people, the opportunities for the members of the community to flourish individually and together become at least as important as the product or services being created.

Ownership will not be approached in the same way. After all, few would want to own a community, or be in a community owned by others. And a community is more than a workplace. A community is an integrated system of relationships. We believe that whole personhood and peer relationships are the basis of authentic community—a communion of whole people.

Carolyn Shaffer and Kristin Anundsen in their book, *Creating Community Anywhere,* talk about community as a dynamic whole that emerges when a group of people participate in common practices; depend on one another; identify themselves as something larger than the sum of their individual relationships; and commit themselves for the long term to their own, one another's and the group's well-being.

They believe a conscious community focuses on internal dynamics and external tasks, and attends to the whole system—individual and group development, process as well as task, interaction with larger communities. They see a conscious community characterized by openness, fluidity, diversity, role-sharing, use of group skills and regular renewal. The values of people who are in a community are trust, honesty, compassion and respect.

In her book, *Swans and Angels,* Patricia Ellis says that you find endless opportunities to grow spiritually in a community because there are constant choices: to love or to hold back, to give more or to fear more. "Paying attention to 'even the dull and ignorant' is hard work. But everywhere the message is the same: in the Bible, the prophets, the esoteric teachings, St. Francis, even in the Desiderata. In a community, we can commit ourselves to behaving in a loving way, to supporting each other's growth, appreciating that it's often uncomfortable."

If you believe that people can be intrinsically bad, that one rotten apple will destroy a whole barrel, that people can't be trusted, that the world is about every person for him- or herself, then the organization as a community will not be for you. And, because we are talking about beliefs and values, it is important to acknowledge that no one knows the full truth on this subject. You can find plenty of supporting evidence no matter what you believe. Your beliefs are valid and so are ours.

But for those people who do want to live by co-operative, inclusive values, the workplace as a community becomes an important possibility. And, if it is possible, we believe it is up to us to find out how to make it happen. This involves finding models that already work and, if there aren't any, inventing them.

A PEER COMMUNITY

We see the peer organization becoming a peer community. The whole will be important and so will the parts. An alignment between the aspirations of the individuals and the development of the organization as a whole will occur. This alignment on the development or future of the organization will keep people working together, along with the strength of the relationships they develop. Respect for individual difference and autonomy will allow individuals to be whole.

How would a peer organization be structured? The structure will be led by its purpose. It might resemble a set of intersecting circles (teams) and dotted lines, representing a co-operative, dynamic body in which each person or team shares information and responsibility with others. At the same time, accountability will be clear and, within that, specific outcomes will be promised.

People will be encouraged to do what they are best at and what is in line with their interests. Assistance, support and coaching will be readily available. If a person is unable to meet the criteria for a particular job, every effort will be made to create or find another inside the organization.

Career development will become *person* development, and the needs of the organization will be balanced against the needs of the individuals in it. Communication will be open, relationships will be developed, emotions will be expressed in safe ways, and criticism will be clear and valued.

Each person will be encouraged to express his or her individuality, and differences that exist will be celebrated for enhancing the richness of the whole. Workplaces will acknowledge that people have families and other relationships that are as important to them as their jobs. Work practices and policies will reflect this.

Life and work are not separate concepts, and personal lives spill over into working time. There will be an understanding that collective decision-making is easier if there are regular renewal sessions to improve teamwork, clarify values and re-establish the organization's vision and mission. Major shareholders, and thus the owners, of the organization will be the core people in it. Resources and profits will be shared. There will be affirming, acknowledging and leaving processes, and an acknowledgment that aspirations change and the organization cannot always accommodate everyone's needs.

The organization will recognize its responsibility to the wider community and to the planet, and will involve itself in initiatives and partnerships to enhance life. This will also be reflected in its code of ethics.

A "BEING" ORGANIZATION

What might an organization look like if it is based within the domain of being rather than doing?

In such an organization, people would dedicate time to paying attention to what is going on inside and around them in the moment ("presencing themselves") and attuning with others. People would align themselves around a purpose in which they believed and that would call them forth to action. They would be connected with others through technology and psychic means.

They would use their intuitive and creative capacities as part of their work. They would network and share information with others of like mind. The organization might have no formal structure and no strategic plan. The future would be uncovered and moved into line with the organization's purpose. Does this sound utopian? Perhaps. However, there are already organizations working in this way, at least in part.

WHO WILL ESTABLISH THESE ORGANIZATIONS?

To attract the kind of highly skilled, creative people ("knowledge workers") that organizations need to be successful in many industries requires more than money alone. Some people are just not willing to sell their time any more for a high-stress, highly paid but "not-whole" life. Many are leaving the traditional workforce and establishing other ways of working. These people, like you and us, are likely to be the people who establish the new kinds of organizations.

MIXED ORGANIZATIONS

Efforts to mix the new-paradigm, peer organizations with the old-paradigm model can work—up to a point. But it is like grafting an orange-tree branch onto an apple tree: The two ways of being are distinct and different, and the interface will be difficult and lead to incongruities that cannot be resolved.

This book is aimed at increasing access to co-operative skills so that more organizations can have a real choice as to the way in which they will work.

Organizational transformation

You may be reading this book because you feel dissatisfied with the environment in which you work. You may feel constrained by it, uncomfortable in it, disappointed in it. You may openly dislike or hate it.

You may be working on your own personal development and want to be in an environment that supports the position you have taken. Reading this book may have helped you develop these thoughts and feelings. You may now have a clearer idea of what is not working and why.

But how will this knowledge help you? Probably it will make you feel more dissatisfied initially. But now you may have a glimpse of a different kind of organization, one that is more like your ideal.

CHANGING AN ORGANIZATION

How can you change the organization you are in to be more like your ideal? You may be inclined to dash back to work and start making suggestions about what you and others can do differently.

This is what happens after people read a good book or take a training course. They come back all fired up with new ideas and try to implement them. It's not impossible, but it's often difficult to bring about change in this way. Why? Because organizations already have a way of being—a set structure, systems and practices that support how they already are and a written or unwritten culture to keep everything in place. So the newly trained person gets disheartened after a while and stops trying.

Even if lots of people take the same training courses and support one another in this effort, it can still be hard to effect real change. Why? Because the training is usually specific and addresses particular aspects, such as performance management, communication or teamwork. The organization is a whole, complete in itself. Altering one or some parts of it does not necessarily work. The organizational "intelligence" will be receiving mixed messages. For example, teamwork may sit uneasily alongside a hierarchical structure for managers who are suddenly required to become team leaders.

CHANGE FROM THE TOP
Some consultants are sure that real change must come from the top. As the instigator and champion of change, the chief executive has the authority to implement changes so they stick. Sometimes this works well, but it needs a participatory leadership style rather than imposition from the top. Imposed change does not create powerful peer relationships.

People also need a lot of reassurance that the change is for the good of all. We can all think of many examples of change in recent times that lead to "downsizing," with lots of people being fired from or phased out of their workplace.

INTERNAL CATALYST
Others believe that being a long-term, internal agent for change is the way to go: the catalyst or 007 approach. To take on this role, you need to have strong external and internal networks. This approach can effectively change an organization, but it is an exhausting way and usually leads to burnout sooner or later. And when you leave, the changes are likely to disappear gradually.

WORKPLACE REFORM
Workplace reform is a popular approach to change at the moment. Often it involves establishing close alliances between management and unions,

and setting up vertical-slice change teams representing all levels of the organization, with the sponsorship of the CEO. This method of managing change can be effective and is worth a try. Organizations supporting this change are available in some areas.

Workplace reform usually works by introducing change incrementally. There is little impetus to alter the ownership of the organization radically or challenge the union/management partnership.

How can an organization be changed to be truly congruent with peer relatedness? This is the first hurdle to cross. Are you talking about change, incremental improvement, the continuous-quality-improvement approach, or do you want transformation? Change can happen in the above ways, but is this really what is needed? We suggest more than this.

TRANSFORMATION

This book is about transformation into a new paradigm of being, what we call "whole personhood." How can this take place?

At some of our workshops we examine the opportunities people have to bring about organizational transformation from within the organization, through understanding and by putting the concepts in this book into practice using the applications contained in Part Two.

Often, highly skilled people are in tears when they describe the personal cost to themselves and their wholeness extracted in the course of performing in their well-paid positions within traditional organizations. For some, the cost is too high. Not uncommonly, we get calls from participants after our courses telling us they have resigned from their jobs.

THE ZENERGY STORY

We too grew tired and burned-out trying to change the big organizations of which we were part. We wanted to try something different. We wanted to find a way to work co-operatively, as peers.

Our company, Zenergy, began in 1992 with three of us. Our business is to develop new ways for people to work together through facilitation, mediation, consulting and training. We started as equal shareholders within a limited-liability company structure.

We found strategic- and business planning were useful tools. We developed systems and adopted the latest computer technology, Internet and mobile phones. We didn't do much marketing because word of mouth seemed to be effective enough to keep us going. We sorted out what taxes to pay and by when.

We thought a lot about our purpose, our vision and our values. We used the image of a boat quite extensively as an image of our journey. We developed our first strategic plan on a catamaran, using a facilitator to take us through the process. We progressed, faltered, picked ourselves up and started to find our niche as facilitators, consultants, authors and facilitator trainers. The mechanics of running our own business took work, but was not too difficult.

PATTERNS FROM THE OLD PARADIGM

Our preconditioned patterns were difficult right from the start. They came back to haunt us! All our workplace learning had come from the old paradigm. That was what we knew, and our automatic reactions tended to come from there. We had either been managers or had been managed by others.

We each had to learn to manage ourselves and provide space for the others to manage themselves. We had to stop projecting onto one another. We had to unlearn patterns of rescuer, intimidator and victim that we were scarcely aware we had taken on.

We found this interpersonal learning the most challenging by far. Some patterns were so deep they seemed intractable. We all wanted to give up at times. Our friendships became strained, too. We stopped wanting to spend social time together. We moaned about one another, just like in the old paradigm. It was a steep learning curve to which we were fortunately all committed. We were unwilling not to be successful. And we had to solve our interpersonal issues because this is, after all, what we were all about. It was discouraging and hard to admit our problems at times. At times we sought help from outside facilitators and consultants.

We began to introduce practices that helped us. Our creation meeting worked, getting us started on a high note at the beginning of each week.

We invented themes for the week that reminded us to be aware—themes such as "watching our patterns with interest" and "bringing forth sparkling resonance"—wrote these up in the office and shared them with others. We held a completion meeting to end the week on a positive note, although we had to learn that getting to completion really meant that there was nothing at all to moan about afterwards. Our business meetings continued to be hard for a long time, because we tended to fall into our patterns over and over. In the end we introduced attunements (see page 53) at the beginning and this helped.

We learned we needed to be rigorous with ourselves in meeting commitments. We learned to be honest on a new, deeper level and to say what was going on with us. We learned to stop trying to change one another and to allow space for one another's differences. We celebrated successes with parties, book launchings and a ball celebrating magnificence at a top hotel.

We attracted lots of people interested in what we were doing. They mostly inspired us to keep going. Some wanted to work with us. We created a core group of the most committed people. And we identified a wider community of clients, course graduates and others interested in what we were up to.

We learned to create clarity and contracts. We created partnerships with other people who inspired us. We began to value the different contributions that we each made and also to value where the gaps were. We tried sharing our earnings and it seemed to work. We realized that we could not work together and write the books together without close co-operation. So we created stakes that were too high for us to be willing to fail. We realized that being in business is a long-term commitment—like marriage, but without the sex. And we are still learning, day by day, inch by inch.

TRANSFORMATION STARTS WITH OURSELVES

What we have basically learned from our work is that creating a new-paradigm organization requires hard work and commitment. It requires being willing to transform ourselves every day if necessary. It is not a journey for the faint-hearted.

There is no recipe for transforming your organization. We hope that the ideas in this book as a whole will stimulate your thinking through a better understanding of the issues. Whether you are looking to transform an existing organization or start a new one, remember to start with and keep working on *yourself*. And we wish you all the best, because what we are doing together is important for the whole world.

BEING PART OF A WORLD CONVERSATION

If you would like to be part of a world conversation about creating new-paradigm organizations, we invite you to contact us (see page 256).

Processes
for
Co-operacy

1 ROUNDS

PURPOSE:	To encourage participation and ensure everyone has an opportunity to be heard.
FOR:	Groups.
ROLES:	Facilitator, timekeeper.
MATERIALS:	White board or large sheets of paper, marker pens.
TIME:	2 or 3 minutes per person, plus 10 minutes for introduction and completion.

INTRODUCTION:

This is a basic technique for groups to use to explore an issue initially, or to use after an issue has been discussed and there is still no clarity. This technique will bring out a range of views in conflict resolution. Its power lies in being a group technique. By hearing everyone's viewpoints, people may change their own, especially if the exercise continues for more than one round. As with all techniques and exercises, begin by describing the process and getting group agreement for it.

PROCESS FOR A STRUCTURED ROUND:

STEP 1: Identify the issue or topic clearly, and perhaps write it down.

STEP 2: Each group member in turn speaks without being interrupted and without response or comment. Others give full attention to the speaker. The timekeeper announces when each person's time is up. Members may skip their turn if they do not wish to contribute. At first you may need to coach participants not to interrupt or respond out of turn. You may need to gently encourage shy members to speak.

159

STEP 3:   At the end of the round, the facilitator summarizes the range of views, including the main points of similarity and difference, and checks this with the group. If the aim is to seek agreement, the facilitator may check out emerging agreements with the group. It is helpful to note the key words or ideas expressed by each member, as well as emerging agreements.

STEP 4:   To complete the process, agree on and record any action. If clarity has not been reached, a second or third round may be needed to see if people's views have changed or developed.

PROCESS FOR AN UNSTRUCTURED ROUND:
An unstructured round is conducted in the same way as a structured round, except there is no prearranged order of speaking. Each person may speak only once during a round. Unstructured rounds work well with more experienced groups.

VARIATIONS:
- Do not impose time limits on speakers.
- Follow the round with a general discussion or dialog. (See chapter 15, *Peer inquiry*, "Strategic dialog.")
- If the group is large, divide it into subgroups of from 3 to 8 people and have them use rounds. Have the subgroups report back to the whole group.

2 BRAINSTORMING

PURPOSE:	To generate a large number of ideas quickly and to encourage creativity and flexible thinking.
FOR:	Pairs, groups.
ROLES:	Facilitator, recorder(s).
MATERIALS:	White board or large sheets of paper, marker pens.
TIME:	Choose a specific amount of time, say 5 or 10 minutes.

PROCESS:

State the issue to be brainstormed. Ask people to say whatever comes into their heads *without censorship and as fast as possible*. Write down all ideas. You will probably need two note-takers to catch all the ideas expressed. Notice how people are inspired by others, and encourage this. Suggest they be more outrageous. Make sure people *do not evaluate or comment on* others' ideas. If participants are sluggish, ask them to stand or hop on one foot.

VARIATION:

Choose a random factor, such as a word from a randomly opened dictionary, and use this word as a key for further brainstorming. For example: *"The issue is peer relationships. The random word is 'pink.' Now use the word 'pink' to spark ideas related to peer relationships."*

3 CONTINUUMS

PURPOSE:	To explore and visually rank the range of views on an issue.
FOR:	Groups.
ROLES:	Facilitator.
MATERIALS:	None.
TIME:	10 to 30 minutes.

PROCESS:

STEP 1: Create an imaginary line through the room, either corner-to-corner or lengthwise. One end has a 0% (low) ranking; the other a 100% (high) ranking. Outline the issue under debate and the two extreme positions. Explain that this is an intuitive as well as a rational exercise and needs to be done quietly and thoughtfully.

STEP 2: Have people walk around to get the feel of the continuum and then place themselves where they fit in terms of the issue. They may try out several spots before making a final choice.

STEP 3: Ask them to have a conversation, for about 2 minutes, with the person beside them, explaining why they are on that spot.

STEP 4: Invite participants to share their viewpoint and feelings about the issue with the group.

VARIATIONS:
- A curved line can be used so people can see each other.
- The conversations (Step 3) could take place among the whole group.
- The line can be "folded in half," so that the low and high ends face each other, and conversations then held.

4 WHO ARE OUR PEERS?

PURPOSE:	To explore our belief system regarding peer relationships.
FOR:	Individuals, pairs and groups.
ROLES:	Facilitator or timekeeper.
MATERIALS:	Large sheets of paper, colored marker pens.
TIME:	26 minutes.

PROCESS:

STEP 1:
(5 MINUTES)   Identify particular people you know who are your peers. Make a chart of their relationship to you on a large sheet of paper using symbols, stick figures or names.

STEP 2:
(3 MINUTES)   Identify particular people or groups of people who are not your peers. Record these.

STEP 3:
(3 MINUTES)   How did you select the different groups? Turn this into a statement and write it down.

STEP 4:
(5 MINUTES)   Think about/discuss in pairs these questions: Is there any way that the different groups could become one group of peers? What would this look like? Is there a statement that might describe the new grouping? What is it?

STEP 5:
(10 MINUTES)   If in a group, share your answers with the whole group.

VARIATION: Use the strategic-dialog method to explore this topic. (See chapter 15, *Peer Inquiry*, "Strategic dialog.")

5 CO-OPERATION AND COMPETITION

PURPOSE:	To explore the relationship between competition and co-operation.
FOR:	Groups.
ROLES:	Facilitator.
MATERIALS:	White board, marker pens, materials for a structured activity. (See "Drop the Egg" on the next page, which requires 20 straws, 1 raw egg and 20 inches of tape for each team.)
TIME:	30 minutes.

PROCESS:

STEP 1:
(3 MINUTES)
Form two or more teams of three people, plus two mobile observers. The observers' role is to note the influence of co-operation and competition. Observers do not interact with the teams.

STEP 2:
(12 MINUTES)
Include a structured activity, such as "Drop the Egg."

STEP 3:
(15 MINUTES)
After the activity, debrief with the participants. Include a report from the observers.
How was co-operation present?
Where wasn't it present?
What got in the way?
What influence did competition have on co-operation?
How did that add to or detract from the activity?
What relationship do you see between co-operation and competition?
Have a general discussion and record findings on the white board.

Drop the Egg

GOAL: To design and build a container using only the supplied materials so a raw egg will survive a free fall of about 8 feet onto a hard surface.

TIME: 5 minutes for individual design and 10 minutes to plan and build the container as a team.

RULES: Only these materials may be used: 20 straws, 20 inches of tape, 1 raw egg. To be eligible to win, a team's egg must survive the drop. Boiling the egg or removing its yolk and white is not allowed.

SCORING: 20 points if the egg survives intact, 1 point for every straw not used, 1 point for every inch of tape not used.

6 MINING FOR GOLD

PURPOSE:	To develop listening skills in distinguishing the "gold" in another's speaking.
FOR:	Group or pair.
ROLES:	Facilitator.
MATERIALS:	White board, marker pens.
TIME:	Up to 50 minutes.

BACKGROUND:

This process practices listening for what is behind what someone is saying, using the heart, head, ears and undivided attention; listening for what is not being said; listening with a particular focus, and getting feedback on that. (Extra time is allowed for changing roles and partners.)

PROCESS:

Write down the topics and what to listen for on the white board.

   Concerns—issues, priorities, values
   Commitment—involvement, dedication, intention
   Contribution—offering, sharing
   Magnificence—uniqueness, greatness; where they are outstanding

Outline the process briefly.

STEP 1:
(4 MINUTES)
Working in pairs, participants choose an A and a B. Person A is the listener; person B is the speaker. B speaks on any topic for 2 minutes. (See list of possible topics opposite.) Person A listens with a particular listening focus. The first listening focus is for *concerns* of the speaker. The concerns don't have to be addressed directly but are in the background of what the speaker says. The other three listening focuses are listed above. Person A reflects back the concerns he or she heard for 1 minute. Person B gives feedback on how well he or she was heard for 1 minute.

"Yes, you heard my concerns."
"You recognized concerns that I was unclear about."
"I didn't feel heard."
"You heard some of what I said, and missed . . ."
"You expressed some concerns that don't sound right to me."

STEP 2:   Participants swap roles.

STEP 3:   Participants change partners and continue the process using the other listening focuses.

STEP 4:   In the whole group, discuss what people noticed, learned
(10 MINUTES) and felt. Did you experience being really listened to? Did you feel recognized? What was the experience of being the listener like for you?

POSSIBLE TOPICS:
Any topic will do, especially if the speaker has enthusiasm for it. We find ordinary ones work well. For example:

Family	Favorite activities
Holidays	Starting the day
Housework	Problems
Work	Politics
Relationships	Food

VARIATIONS:
- Do this exercise in two circles, one inside the other. Form pairs, with the inner circle facing out and the outer circle facing in. After the first topic, everyone in the outer circle moves clockwise to form a new pair. After the second topic, people on the inside move counterclockwise. After the third topic the outside circle moves counterclockwise.
- Change the listening focus when pairs swap roles. This will reduce the time of the exercise by half.
- Eliminate one of the listening focuses.

7 Negotiating and contracting with peers

PURPOSE:	This is a model for negotiation with peers.
FOR:	Pairs.
ROLES:	None.
MATERIALS:	Paper, pen.
TIME:	15 to 30 minutes.

PROCESS:

STEP 1:   The person raising the issue, A, requests a conversation with B, the person responding. Person A says what the topic is and asks if person B is available to discuss it immediately.

STEP 2:   Person A states the concern, disagreement or complaint as specifically as possible. For example:
"I have asked to have our team briefing time changed, and we are still having it at 9:00 a.m. Monday."
"You took four telephone calls during our meeting yesterday."

STEP 3:   Both people state what they want:
A: *"I would like the team briefing to be at 4:00 p.m. on Tuesday."*
B: *"I want the briefing to be as early as possible in the week."*
A: *"Please turn off your cell phone when we meet."*
B: *"I need to be available to my clients."*

STEP 4:   Having heard each other's statements, A continues to negotiate:
"Are you willing to take the issue to our next meeting?"
"I am asking for no interruptions. Is there anything else you are willing to do about this?"

STEP 5:   B responds:
            Agreeing: *"Yes, I will do that."*
            Delaying: *"Let me think about that."*
            Disagreeing: *"No, I don't want to change the meeting time."*
            Counter-offering: *"No, but I will discuss it with the team."*
            "I will take messages and return the calls later."

STEP 6:   A responds: *"Yes, that will work for me."*
            "No, that won't work for me."
            If agreement is not reached, A continues to negotiate.
            "Can you suggest something that will meet both our needs?"

STEP 7:   B offers: *"I am happy to decide at the meeting."*
            "I am willing to turn off the phone and check my calls hourly."
            Continue until an agreement is reached.

STEP 8:   A responds: *"I'm willing to try that for a week."*
            "I will need to know your decision tomorrow."

STEP 9:   Acknowledge each other for working with a difficult issue
            and for reaching the current outcome.

Note: If you have difficulty reaching an agreement, refer back to your purpose, commitments or common values. Why is it important to sort out this issue?

Stay with the process, even when it seems tough. Our experience is that you often have to go past the point of thinking you will never reach a solution, that the other person is totally unreasonable, or feeling annoyed and frustrated. This often seems to occur just before an agreement is reached.

If you don't find a win-win outcome, use a facilitator.

8 ACKNOWLEDGMENT

PURPOSE:	To say positive things to each other that have been thought but not stated.
FOR:	Groups.
ROLES:	Facilitator.
MATERIALS:	None.
TIME:	3 minutes per pair, plus 10 minutes in the whole group.

PROCESS:

STEP 1:
(3 MINUTES)
Choose partners. One person starts by acknowledging the other. For example:
"I valued the input you made to our team project."
"I admire the courage you showed in challenging our team."
"I find your comment thought-provoking."
"I enjoy your humor."
The receiver thanks without comment.

STEP 2:
(3 MINUTES)
Find a new partner. Repeat Step 1.

STEP 3:
Continue repeating Step 1 until everyone has had a turn with each other, or as time allows.

STEP 4:
(10 MINUTES)
With the attention of the entire group, check whether anyone has any other acknowledgments to make that may have just occurred to them. Ask for reactions to the process, and thank people for taking part.

PROCESSES FOR WHOLE PERSONHOOD

9 ATTENDING TO ANOTHER

PURPOSE:	To attend to another as a whole being.
FOR:	Groups or pairs.
ROLES:	Facilitator for a group.
MATERIALS:	None.
TIME:	30 minutes.

PROCESS:

STEP 1:
(5 MINUTES)
In pairs, choose an A and a B. Face each other and relax. Then A "attends" to B while B shares an experience. By "attending," we mean in silence, bringing awareness to the wholeness of the other, including spiritual, conceptual, emotional, energetic, physical and intuitive awareness.

STEP 2:
(5 MINUTES)
Starting with B, pairs take turns to share what they noticed.

STEP 3:
(10 MINUTES)
Pairs change roles and repeat Steps 1 and 2.

STEP 4:
(10 MINUTES)
If in a group, bring everyone together and complete the process by sharing in the whole group.

VARIATIONS:
- Repeat exercise with both A and B closing their eyes.
- Extend the time as you feel comfortable, up to 40 minutes.
- Try the exercise in small groups or in the whole group.

171

10 WHOLE-BEING EXPLORATION

PURPOSE:	To explore and develop aspects of whole being.
FOR:	Individuals, pairs and groups.
ROLES:	Facilitator for a group.
MATERIALS:	Paper, colored pens.
TIME:	50 minutes.

PROCESS:

STEP 1:
(10 MINUTES) Use the model "Aspects of whole personhood" on pages 27–29 as a springboard to create your own model of whole being. Draw your own model. Include aspects you feel are important.

STEP 2:
(10 MINUTES) In threes or fours, share your model with others.

STEP 3:
(5 MINUTES) After listening to others you might want to include more aspects in your own model.

STEP 4:
(2 MINUTES) Take another look at your model. Notice any aspects that you are curious about, feel drawn to or want more of. Check for any "shoulds," "oughts" or "musts."

STEP 5:
(5 MINUTES) Choose one aspect and explore it in detail. You may want to use some of these questions to get started:
What drew you to this aspect? What are your thoughts about it? What are your feelings about it? What experiences have you had of this aspect? What further experiences would you like to have? Who would you like to have these experiences with—self, another, group, community?

STEP 6:
(3 MINUTES) Consider these questions: What one thing will you do to develop this aspect? When will you do this?

STEP 7:
(15 MINUTES) Share in the whole group your revised models and/or one decision from this process.

11 WHOLE-PERSON RESOURCES

PURPOSE:	To become aware of your resources for developing as a whole person.
FOR:	Pairs or groups.
ROLES:	Facilitator for a group.
MATERIALS:	Paper, colored pens.
TIME:	40 minutes.

PROCESS:

STEP 1:
(5 MINUTES)
Reflect on when and where you have experienced yourself as a whole person in the following areas. Record these as drawings or words.
By yourself
With another person
With a group or wider community
In nature
With the whole planet
In the spiritual domain as you define it

STEP 2:
(6 MINUTES)
Share with another person (3 minutes each).

STEP 3:
(5 MINUTES)
Having shared these ideas, do any other resources come to mind? Share those. Record them.

STEP 4:
(5 MINUTES)
Bring a number of different aspects of whole being to this question one at a time. What do you notice?

STEP 5:
(4 MINUTES)
Share what you learned in Step 4 in pairs (2 minutes each). Acknowledge the person with whom you have shared.

STEP 6:
(15 MINUTES)
Share what you have discovered in the whole group. Is there anything to say to complete this process?

12 RECREATING WHOLE BEING

PURPOSE:	To recreate whole being.
FOR:	Individuals, pairs or groups.
ROLES:	Facilitator for a group.
MATERIALS:	None.
TIME:	20 minutes.

PROCESS:

STEP 1:
(5 MINUTES)
Use any method to take you into a relaxed state. The process in the box on the next page is one suggestion.

STEP 2:
(5 TO 10 MINUTES)
Notice any thoughts and sensations. Notice thoughts that lead to doing. Notice sensations that take you into being. Keep watching your breathing. Always come back to your breathing when you become distracted by your thoughts.

STEP 3:
(2 MINUTES)
When you are ready to complete this stage, thank yourself for taking time to do this process. Acknowledge all the powerful creative resources that exist within you and within the whole universe.

STEP 4:
(2 MINUTES)
When you are ready, bring yourself slowly out of your relaxed state. Count down slowly from five to one. When you reach one, gradually come back to the room, ready to engage in whatever is ahead of you.

VARIATION:

Use this process in a natural environment, such as a garden. In the meditative state (Step 2) open yourself to nature and being in nature.

To get into a relaxed state

Get into a comfortable position. *(Pause)*

Turn your attention to your breathing. *(Pause)*

Each time you exhale, allow your relaxation to deepen. *(Pause)*

Find a part of your body that is relaxed and allow that relaxation to flow and spread through your whole body. *(Pause)*

Find a part of your body that isn't relaxed and imagine those muscles relaxing. *(Pause)*

Thank yourself for allowing this relaxation and for creating this opportunity.

13 EXPLORING POWER

PURPOSE:	To explore power in a group or organization.
FOR:	Groups or small organizations.
ROLES:	Facilitator.
MATERIALS:	None.
TIME:	25 to 35 minutes.

PROCESS:

STEP 1:
(5 MINUTES)
Invite one group member to form a continuum of the other group members based on how powerful he or she considers each person in the group, using only his or her own perceptions and criteria. Make sure a single line is created. Then ask the group member to put him- or herself in the line. Encourage this person to verbalize the reasons for the placements.

STEP 2:
(5 MINUTES)
Check for comments from the group. Give everyone who wants to a chance to speak.

STEP 3:
(5 MINUTES)
Invite another person to form a continuum in the same way.

STEP 4:
(5 MINUTES)
Check for comments from the group. Give everyone a chance to speak who wants to.

STEP 5:
(5 TO 10 MINUTES)
Continue until each person has had a turn or as time allows. Sometimes you will find there is alignment or that alignment develops.

14 MAPPING POWER

PURPOSE:	To identify where different kinds of power lie in a group.
FOR:	Groups.
ROLES:	Facilitator.
MATERIALS:	Large sheets of paper, marker pens.
TIME:	40 minutes.

PROCESS:

STEP 1:
(5 MINUTES)
Working individually, have each person draw the groups to which they belong on a large sheet of paper. Each group is to be represented by a symbol (circle, or other) and is named.

STEP 2:
(5 MINUTES)
Have participants identify the key roles in each group; for example: chairperson, facilitator, team leader, manager, recorder.

STEP 3:
(10 MINUTES)
Have participants identify where the different kinds of power are in the groups, writing down the names of the people and concentrating on positional or assigned power.
(See chapter 4.)

STEP 4:
(10 MINUTES)
Have participants consider any of the following questions in small groups of three or four:
What patterns do you notice?
What effect does it have if people with positional power also have assigned power?
Are there people in your groups who have more than three kinds of power?
What are your feelings or thoughts about these people?
What kinds of power do you have?
How could you become more powerful in this group?

STEP 5:
(10 MINUTES)
Have participants come back to the large group for sharing.

15 POWER AND MONEY

PURPOSE:	To raise issues that revolve around power and money.
FOR:	Groups of 5 to 8.
ROLES:	Facilitator.
MATERIAL:	Each person needs to provide an amount of money, the amount being decided by the group.
TIME:	30 minutes.

PROCESS:

STEP 1:
(5 MINUTES)

Ask everyone to place their money into a container.

STEP 2:
(10 MINUTES)

Ask the group to decide how this money will be distributed. Put a time limit on this, such as 10 minutes.

STEP 3:
(2 MINUTES)

Have the group distribute the money as agreed.

STEP 4:
(13 MINUTES)

Ask group members to share what they notice from this process. Do this as a round. You may want to use the following questions as a springboard.

What are your thoughts about the process?
What are your feelings?
What are your reactions?
Did you feel powerful?
Did you say what you wanted to say?
After everyone has shared, check if anyone wants to add anything now that they have heard from everyone.
Have the group consider this question:
What have you learned?

16 ALIGNMENT

PURPOSE:	To explore the effect of intentionally aligning on a project.
FOR:	Groups.
ROLES:	Facilitator.
MATERIALS:	Jigsaw puzzle or materials for a simple construction project of your choice.
TIME:	30 minutes.

PROCESS:

STEP 1:
(5 MINUTES)
Without discussing the purpose of the task, ask the group to divide into two groups, and undertake a similar task—for example, a jigsaw puzzle or a simple construction exercise.

STEP 2:
(5 MINUTES)
Stop the process and give each group time to align on a purpose for their activity that the group finds inspiring.

STEP 3:
(10 MINUTES)
Continue the task.

Step 4:
(10 MINUTES)
In the whole group, have members share what they noticed about taking time to align on the task. What are the implications for this group?

17 Yo

PURPOSE:	A ritual to acknowledge alignment.
FOR:	Pairs or groups.
ROLES:	An initiator.
MATERIALS:	None.
TIME:	5 minutes.

BACKGROUND:

This ritual was introduced to us as a process used in the Japanese business environment to recognize that alignment has been reached. It also expresses a commitment—that there will be no going back. If this ritual is being introduced for the first time, the initiator may want to share its background and meaning.

PROCESS:

STEP 1: A group member or the facilitator acknowledges that alignment has been reached and asks if everyone would like to check for group alignment with a brief ritual. If everyone is willing, continue.

STEP 2: Everyone stands or sits a sufficient distance apart to be able to spread their arms out sideways and clap their hands in front of them without touching each other.

STEP 3: With *no leader*, the group simultaneously claps their hands and shouts "yo!" If the *yo* is not simultaneous, the initiator calls for another turn. Identify that this is a new occasion. You may invite people to take a minute to tune in to one another. Be willing to try several times if necessary. We have worked with groups that practice this ritual with their eyes shut.

18 FINDING THE GROUP PURPOSE

PURPOSE:	To align on a group purpose.
FOR:	Groups.
ROLES:	Facilitator.
MATERIALS:	White board, marker pens.
TIME:	30 to 40 minutes.

PROCESS:

STEP 1:
(3 MINUTES)
Introduce the idea of aligning on a group purpose that is specific, short and inspiring. Emphasize that the purpose will tell the group **what** it is going to accomplish, not **how** it will do it.

STEP 2:
(5 MINUTES)
Ask groups of three or four find a sentence or phrase, symbol, drawing, mind map or combination that expresses the purpose of the group. As each group finds its purpose, ask them to write it on the white board.

STEP 3:
(5 TO 15 MINUTES)
With the whole group back together, invite everyone to allow their thinking to extend beyond attachment to their own ideas. This is about working together to achieve an inspirational outcome. Create a group purpose using the ideas already presented as a springboard. It may be that one of those presented, or a combination, is the "one." If no agreement occurs, a new purpose may emerge out of common elements of several suggestions, or someone may have a brainstorm.

STEP 4:
(5 MINUTES)
Write the agreed purpose on the white board. Check for alignment—if alignment is present, people will be "lit up," ready for action. Celebrate!

STEP 5:
(OPTIONAL)
If no aligned purpose is forthcoming, have a session on sharing "withholds" (Process 23). It may be that people have under-lying concerns or there may not be a clear purpose for the group.
(See also Process 42, *Finding the higher purpose.*)

19 GETTING PRESENT

PURPOSE:	To have everyone fully present.
FOR:	Pairs or groups.
ROLES:	Facilitator for a group.
MATERIALS:	None.
TIME:	For task-focused groups, 1 to 5 minutes per person.

BACKGROUND:

This exercise provides a space for everyone at a meeting to say and do anything they need to be fully present. Time taken to do this process is never wasted because it frees the group to work synergistically and with velocity.

For in-depth development and highly creative groups, this process will take however long it takes.

The time it takes will vary depending on the purpose, the balance of task and process in the group, individual awareness levels and the level of commitment to group consciousness.

PROCESS:

STEP 1: People sit in a circle so that they can see and hear each other. A facilitator is chosen and negotiates the time frame. The facilitator invites everyone to share in turn, uninterrupted, any little bothers, concerns, distractions, events and incidents that are on their mind or in the background. For example:

"I'm giving a presentation to a client this afternoon and I feel nervous."

"I broke an expensive piece of equipment yesterday and I haven't reported it yet. It's on my mind."

"My daughter had a baby last night. It's our first grandchild."

"I had an argument with my partner this morning and I'm still angry."

"I'm uncomfortable with Bill (also in the group). We had a disagreement yesterday. I request a clearing session [time to clear the air with Bill] now or at an arranged time outside the group."

Ask everyone to give full attention to the speaker. As facilitator you may coach people if they appear stuck. Interventions could include:

"Is there any action you want to take?"

"Are you present now?"

"Is there anything else you want to say about that?"

STEP 2:   After everyone has spoken, declare the round complete.

VARIATIONS:

- Invite people to share any insights or reflections that will deepen the unity of the group.
- Include dreams, coincidences or other phenomena.
- People speak in pairs or threes and then share briefly in the whole group.
- There is a specific time for each person, and a timekeeper is chosen to monitor this.
- Have no limits on time and work with each person until they are fully "present" (see page 30).
- Request that people get present (see page 30) before they enter the room. Have a rigorous person at the door to check for presence before they enter (see page 30).
- Invent a ritual to acknowledge everyone's presence.

20 CREATION MEETING

PURPOSE:	To start the week powerfully.
FOR:	Two or more people.
ROLES:	Facilitator or timekeeper.
MATERIALS:	Diaries.
TIME:	1 hour.

PROCESS:

STEP 1:
(3 MINUTES)
Everyone meets in a comfortable space, such as at a round table, where they can see each other. Tea and coffee are available. Someone offers to facilitate.

STEP 2:
(UP TO 40 MINUTES)
Each person has a turn to:
- Share to be present (see page 30).
- Catch up with one another on personal news.
- Reflect on the main tasks and events for the week ahead. This can include concerns, challenges and requests of others relating to the week.

STEP 3:
(5 MINUTES)
An attunement ritual, such as a period of silence with or without joining hands, is held.

STEP 4:
(5 MINUTES)
A theme for the group is developed together. We use themes that:
- Inspire each person
- Call everyone to be in action
- Reflect what we are working on collectively
- We can all align on

STEP 5:
(2 MINUTES)
A completing ritual, such as joining hands for a few minutes or a short period of silence.

STEP 6:   Individuals set times for meetings with one another. The
(5 MINUTES) theme is written up in prominent places—for example, on a
             white board and on computer screen-savers.

VARIATIONS:
- Use this process to begin a project or workshop.
- Subgroups may meet for specific purposes after the whole-group meeting.
- Have the meeting without a facilitator.

21 CULTURE-SETTING

PURPOSE:	To design how you will work together.
FOR:	Groups.
ROLES:	Facilitator, recorder.
MATERIALS:	White board or large sheet of paper, marker pens.
TIME:	30 to 40 minutes.

BACKGROUND:

This is a process for choosing with awareness how you will work together. It will include the beliefs, values and practices that become the agreed basis for all interactions within the group. Before this process is undertaken it is necessary to get clear about your group or organization purpose. The culture then has a context and will be appropriate for your purpose. For an organization it is also helpful to have developed a vision statement.

PROCESS:

STEP 1:
(10 MINUTES)

Invite everyone to sit so that they can see each other. Ask one or two volunteers to write down what is expressed. Then ask for a brainstorm on:

"How do we want to work together?"
Welcome and record all suggestions. Do not discuss the suggestions. Suggestions may include specific "ground rules" such as:

Be on time.
Personal information remains confidential.
Take your complaint to the person it belongs to.
Speak only for yourself.

—or more general value statements such as:

Feelings are fine.
Participate wholeheartedly.
Vulnerability is recognized as an opportunity for growth.
Support each other to develop skills.

STEP 2:	When all suggestions have been offered, check for overlap. If
(5 MINUTES)	in doubt, check the suggestions with the people who
	proposed them.

STEP 2:
(5 MINUTES) When all suggestions have been offered, check for overlap. If in doubt, check the suggestions with the people who proposed them.

STEP 3:
(5 TO 10 MINUTES) Ask: *"Are there any suggestions with which you don't agree?"* Discuss these. Ask the person who proposed the suggestion to say why it is important to them. Work to reach agreement and be inclusive. If agreement cannot be reached, however, ask if the person's need can be met through some other suggestion already on the board. Keep negotiating until everyone is satisfied.

STEP 4:
(5 MINUTES) Check that everyone is in agreement with the culture. Check the mood of the group. If group members are not "lit up," something is missing from the culture or something is in it on which the group is not aligned. Either keep going or reassure the group that the culture is a "living document" that can be reviewed whenever anyone wants to do so. Then ask: *"Does everyone agree that this is the way we will work together?"* Go around the group to get individual agreement. See that everyone nods or says "yes."

STEP 5:
(2 MINUTES) Ask for someone to arrange to make a copy large enough for everyone to see easily.

STEP 6:
(2 MINUTES) Check for alignment with a "Yo" (Process 17) or some ritual completion.

NOTE: 1. The culture statement needs to be posted where it is visible to everybody. It needs to be referred to when anyone thinks it may not be being kept, when someone's "alarm bells" start to ring, and when someone is uncomfortable about something: *"What do we say in our culture about this?"*

2. It can be left as an open document to be added to as awareness grows.

22 BEING WITH A GROUP

PURPOSE:	To experience being fully present to yourself and other members of the group.
FOR:	Groups.
ROLES:	Facilitator.
MATERIALS:	None.
TIME:	25 minutes.

PROCESS:

STEP 1:
(3 MINUTES)

Invite participants to stand or sit in a circle, facing one another. Ask them to become aware of their breathing. If they are sitting, ask that they do not cross their arms or legs. Have them center their attention in their belly and imagine they are like a tree with a root system deep within the ground and branches reaching toward the sky. Ask them to be aware of their physical body, their energy and the space around them.

STEP 2:
(3 MINUTES)

Encourage participants to let themselves become aware of the other group members. Ask them to give their attention to each group member in turn using soft eyes (slightly out of focus). Have them move their attention around the group, looking at other people but not engaging with them. Encourage them to continue paying attention to their breathing, keeping it relaxed and deep.

STEP 3:
(3 MINUTES)

Invite participants to pay attention to the whole presence of each person, being aware of their physical body and the space around them. Ask them to keep their attention moving so that they become present to everyone in the group.

STEP 4: Invite participants to become aware of the group as a whole,
(3 MINUTES) expanding their peripheral vision so that, as their attention
moves around the group, they are aware of the whole group
at the edges of their vision.

STEP 5: Ask participants to continue this process with their eyes shut,
(3 MINUTES) still moving around the group with their attention.
Encourage them to go around to each member in the group,
noticing what they recall of them. Emphasize that they can
take their time with this.

STEP 6: Ask participants to open their eyes and continue to be with
(3 MINUTES) each person and the group. Did they recall where people
were seated? What they were wearing? Whom did they not
remember? Whom did they remember? What else did they
notice?

STEP 7: Invite people to share what they noticed with the group. Did
(7 MINUTES) they notice anything about the energy of individuals or the
group as a whole?

VARIATIONS:
• Practice this exercise while holding hands. Be present to the energy in
the group and between hands.

  Note: In the Southern Hemisphere, people in a circle tend to hold
  hands with the left-hand palm up, right-hand palm down (or "thumbs
  left," as some people say). It seems that the energy is better felt this
  way. We have been told that people in the Northern Hemisphere tend
  to hold hands with the left-hand palm down and right-hand palm up.
• Immediately after this exercise, encourage the group to chant or sing
together.

23 SHARING WITHHOLDS

Lack of energy usually has to do with a failure to communicate. Withholds—the thoughts we keep to ourselves—usually have to do with judgments about ourselves, others, or what is happenening in the group. We withhold out of fear. There needs to be a high level of trust in a group, a climate of generous listening, before sharing withholds is possible.

Shared withholds are about speaking *our* truth but they are not **the** truth. It is important for everyone involved to understand this. When expressed, withholds can be taken to heart or simply acknowledged and let go of if they are unhelpful to the recipient. They often say more about the giver than the receiver—so keep an open mind.

The person receiving the withheld communication acknowledges it by thanking the giver. Avoid responding any further, because it can lead to self-justification and devalue the courage it takes to share these blocked or hidden thoughts.

PURPOSE:	To free group energy.
FOR:	Pairs or groups.
ROLES:	Facilitator for a group.

SHARING WITHHOLDS ABOUT OURSELVES

TIME: 30 minutes to 1 hour.

PROCESS:
Have a round in which each person shares something they have been withholding from the group about themselves—something they have been thinking but not saying. Suggest some starting phrases such as:
   "You would understand me more if you knew . . ."
   "Sometimes I . . . (behavior) when I feel . . . (feeling)."
   "I would contribute more to the group if I . . ."

This process works best if you go around the group several times until people are brave enough to say what they are really withholding.

SHARING WITHHOLDS ABOUT ANOTHER

TIME: 35 minutes or more.

PROCESS:

STEP 1:   Discuss the purpose of sharing withholds. As well as
(10 MINUTES)   withholding about ourselves, another source of low energy is often things that we are not saying to each other. Some of these can be acknowledging, such as:

"I think you presented your report last week really well."
"I admire the way you handled our meeting this week."

Or challenging, such as:

"I thought you dominated our last meeting, and at the time I was annoyed about it."
"I haven't heard you saying anything at our team meetings, and I wonder why."

Check to see if people are willing to try this exercise. Get agreement before continuing.

STEP 2:   Standing up, invite participants to move to one person at a
(15 MINUTES)   time and share anything that they have been withholding. The person who receives the withhold makes no response other than "Thank you." (If appropriate, keep going as long as energy is high.)

STEP 3:   Return to the whole group, and ask if there is anything to
(10 MINUTES)   share about the process or how they are feeling (not the content of any withhold). Check the energy level.

(CONTINUED)

SHARING GROUP WITHHOLDS

TIME: 30 minutes.

PROCESS:

STEP 1:
(5 MINUTES)

Introduce the idea of sharing withholds, suggesting you do this in the whole group.

STEP 2:
(10 MINUTES)

Set up an unstructured round. Do not allow anyone to respond to the withholds or start a discussion.

"If I could change one thing in the group it would be . . ."
"What upsets me about this group is . . ."

STEP 3:
(15 MINUTES)

At the end of the round, see if any themes have emerged and if anyone wants their issue discussed.

SHARING WITHHOLDS

After practicing the above exercises, you may want to combine them to share any withholds. This may take between 10 and 30 minutes.

24 GETTING COMPLETE

This and the following exercise are powerful as ongoing processes. They are also essential for completing a project.

PURPOSE:	To complete with a group or a project.
FOR:	Groups.
ROLES:	Facilitator or timekeeper.
MATERIALS:	None.
TIME:	Up to 5 minutes per person.

PROCESS:
Ask each person in turn these three questions:

QUESTION 1:
"What do you need to complete your involvement with this group?"
or:
"What do you need to say to be complete?"

QUESTION 2:
"Is there anything else?" "Any bothers, thoughts, feelings, unmet expectations, requests, promises?" (Suggest as appropriate.)
"If there is anything you might say to someone after the group is over, I request that you say it now."

The person should think carefully to see if they have left any "baggage" behind—anything they would like to say to someone else after the group.

QUESTION 3:
"Are there acknowledgments anyone would like to make to themselves or others?"

The only response from those acknowledged is "Thank you."

25 COMPLETION MEETING

PURPOSE:	To complete activity with a group or a project. Use this process when you are more familiar with getting complete.
FOR:	Groups.
ROLES:	Facilitator or timekeeper.
MATERIALS:	None.
TIME:	Up to 5 minutes per person.

PROCESS:
Each person in turn reviews their part in the project, including:

- What they have achieved.
- Any commitments made that were not completed—new commitments can be made or agreements revoked.
- Any interpersonal, small problems are expressed and cleared up.
- Any acknowledgment of self or others is given.

Anyone may ask for feedback on work done. The facilitator may check to see if that person has said everything he or she wants to say.

VARIATION:
This process is powerful as an ongoing process to use at the end of each week.

26 CLEARING PROCESS

CLEARING GUIDELINES

Indications that a clearing session is needed are:

- A vague feeling of discomfort with someone or the group.
- A reluctance to participate fully in the relationship or the group.
- Avoiding eye contact with someone, or a number of people.
- Not having much fun together.
- Low energy.
- Often feeling irritable with someone or a number of people.
- A certainty that you are right and someone else is wrong.
- A feeling of resignation or hopelessness about your relationship with someone or the group.
- A feeling of alienation from others.
- Yawning and suddenly feeling tired.
- Inability to reach agreement on a number of issues.

Clearing processes must always be voluntary. Most people have little or no experience of being "clear" with people, and react to each other out of old patterns—often from their parents and family. So these new processes are revolutionary and, if used regularly, will alter the way we relate to each other. The main thing to watch for is people projecting distress onto others (making it their fault) and stopping the process too soon, before all have reached "the bottom of the well" and are clear.

(CONTINUED)

PURPOSE:	To become clear with yourself and another person.
FOR:	Pairs.
ROLES:	Facilitator (optional).
MATERIALS:	None.
TIME:	Variable, 10 to 30 minutes, but it can take longer.

PROCESS:

STEP 1:   The person who recognizes he or she is not clear invites the other person to have a clearing session.

"I'm feeling uncomfortable around you. I'm not sure what it's about. Can we meet and have a clearing session? Are you available now?"

If the other person is willing but currently unavailable, arrange a time and place. You may agree to have a facilitator present or call on one if you get stuck.

STEP 2:   Start the session by each declaring what you are committed to in the relationship, for yourself and the other person. For example:

"I am committed to our good working relationship (or friendship) and want to be relaxed around you. And I want you to be comfortable around me, too."

STEP 3:   The initiator describes the feeling or behavior that he or she has noticed in him- or herself. Try to identify the incident. There is one, always. If there is more than one, choose the most recent.

"I noticed I was uncomfortable (or annoyed) when . . . happened."
"And what is underneath that is . . ."
"And the feelings I have about that are . . ."

The hard things to say are usually feelings that we don't like to admit to others. They often seem petty and despicable—such as feelings of jealousy, anger, meanness (not wanting to lend or share things), being invaded or taken advantage of or being subjected to too many demands. The feelings don't fit with our image of ourselves as generous and tolerant. They often seem to relate more to our childhood than to the present.

Own all the feelings as your own and tell the other person what behavior triggered you, without judgment of right or wrong, good or bad, of either yourself or the other person. This part is often the hardest. You may also be reminded of past incidents with that person or someone else when something similar happened. Say this, too.

"Another situation like it that I remember is . . ."
"When that happened I felt . . ."

Keep speaking, uninterrupted, until you can go no further.

STEP 4:   When the initiator has said all he or she has to say, the other person has a turn to say how it is for him or her and to respond to the initiator. Say everything that is on your mind.

STEP 5:   Repeat Steps 3 and 4 until you are both empty.
You will know when clearing is complete, when you reach the bottom of the well, because you will feel empty, complete—there is nothing left to say. You are freed to *be* with the other person. You will have space to appreciate, recognize and love him or her.

STEP 6:   Silence for a few minutes can be healing.

(CONTINUED)

STEP 7:   There may be requests and promises you both want to make at the end.

"I request that when that situation happens again you . . . (be specific)."

Note: If you get stuck, either person may call time-out and re-negotiate to meet later with a facilitator. Relationships, particularly close ones, will bring up old unhealed patterns from the past, many having to do with our parents and siblings. You almost certainly will have touched on deep hurts, perhaps without being aware of them.

STEP 8:   When the process is complete, thank one another and acknowledge your own and their courage and magnificence.

VARIATION:
The speaker makes one point at a time. After each point, the listener reflects back the essence of what they heard as a checking process. The speaker needs to be satisfied with the reflection before the other person has a turn. Use this variation for all or part of the time. It is most useful when one or both people are "becoming triggered." When we are triggered, we tend to remember only the trigger phrase and not the other things that were said.

27 GROUP CLEARING

If most of the group is involved, you may choose to have a clearing session (preferably immediately) or schedule a special group clearing session if it appears likely that more time is needed.

Note: If the group is co-operative, it will usually have a commitment to reach agreement. If the group is hierarchical or ad hoc, it will now need to consider whether it is prepared to make a commitment to get clear and reach agreement. Group members will have to consider whether there is sufficient safety (confidentiality and power balance) for people to allow themselves to be vulnerable. This process is not appropriate for uncommitted groups. Read clearing guidelines (page 195) and Process 26 as preparation for this session.

PURPOSE:	To clear away anything that is getting in the way of the group fulfilling its purpose.
FOR:	Groups.
ROLES:	Facilitator.
MATERIALS:	White board or large sheet of paper, marker pens.
TIME:	Variable; 40 minutes to 3 hours. There must be a commitment to see the process through.

PROCESS:

STEP 1: Declare a breakdown in the group: *"Stop. This is not working.*
(2 MINUTES) *Let's have a clearing session."* Check for agreement to begin the clearing process. If there is agreement, continue.

STEP 2: Have someone give the purpose and the vision of the group:
(5 MINUTES) *"Our purpose is . . . Our vision is . . ."*

If the purpose and vision are unclear, this may be the issue.

(CONTINUED)

Step 3:
(10 to 30 minutes)
Invite participants to identify what is getting in the way of their full participation in the group.
"What's getting in the way for me is . . ."

Take turns in uninterrupted rounds. Listen to one another generously. Continue with the rounds until the group reaches the bottom of the well, as described in Process 26. Encourage group members to own their own feelings and thoughts rather than project them on to others. If requests are made in the rounds, write them down on the white board to address after the rounds are completed.

Step 4:
(10 to 20 minutes)
When the rounds have been completed, ask for any further specific requests and add these to the white board. Address requests one at a time. Have everyone accept, decline or make a counter-offer. If no counter-offer is acceptable, ask the whole group to suggest solutions.

Step 5:
(15 minutes)
If the group cannot come to an agreement, it is likely that the group is still not clear.

Step 6:
Go back to the beginning of this exercise and repeat the process. Do not finish until the group is complete.

Step 7:
If you have repeated the exercise three times and the group is still not clear, ask each person to choose whether or not to remain and recommit themselves to the group. Provide a generous opening for people to choose.

28 STRATEGIC PLANNING

PURPOSE:	To create a strategic plan for an organization with some stability—that is, with an ability to plan at least a year ahead.
FOR:	Organizations.
ROLES:	*Facilitator.* It is best to use an outside facilitator to develop a strategic plan. The facilitator will guide the process and leave all participants free to become involved in developing content. (The facilitator may use a different model than the one below.) Discuss the model and agree on it before you begin. It is not a good idea for the chief executive to take on the facilitator role because the combination of established and assigned power is likely to inhibit the other participants.
	Note-taker. All findings are written down.
MATERIALS:	Large sheets of paper or a white board; marker pens.
TIME:	Unlimited.

THE MODEL:

Strategic planning begins with the large picture and gradually moves towards the detail, somewhat like a funnel. Each step is essential because it leads directly to the next. This model provides just the bare bones, rather than the details of each step.

PROCESS:

STEP 1: VISION

A word picture of the future you seek to create, described in the present tense, as if it were happening now. Think ahead three to five years at least and imagine what will be happening, as if you were returning from a space trip. What do you see? This vision may include a drawing as well as words. A vision answers the question: Where will we be in five years' time?

STEP 2: MISSION OR PURPOSE

A short inspirational statement, easy to remember, that describes the business the organization is engaged in. The statement captures the essence of the vision and serves as a guiding star. A sentence of 12 words or less is a good guide for length. Everyone must be able to remember it. A longer mission is called a *mission statement* or *statement of intent*. A mission may remain with the company for 10 years or more.

STEP 3: VALUES

A statement of key values, principles or philosophy that describes why the organization wants to do this work. It answers the question: *Why do we want to do this?* Values describe how you intend to operate on a day-to-day basis as you pursue your vision. A set of values may include how you want to behave with each other, how you expect to regard your customers, community and vendors. Values are best expressed as behavior—what will others see you doing?

STEP 4: STRENGTHS, WEAKNESSES, OPPORTUNITIES AND THREATS

Often called a SWOT analysis, this process looks at the strengths and weaknesses of the organization and the opportunities and threats in the external environment.

STEP 5: CRITICAL FACTORS

An identification of the critical factors that will determine the success or failure of the organization. The critical factors come out of the SWOT analysis. A very close look at the SWOT analysis results will lead to the identification of three to six key factors that must be addressed if the organization is to achieve success or avoid failure.

(CONTINUED)

STEP 6: GOALS

Goals set the direction of the organization. They very often come from the critical factors (Step 5) and are short statements of direction containing only one idea. The goals are usually for a two- to three-year span and are reviewed every year. They answer the question: *Where are we going now?*

STEP 7: STRATEGIES AND PRIORITIES

Strategies are developed to support each goal. These can be brainstormed, then discussed in depth and prioritized. Key strategies can then be chosen that will form the basis for the next step. The questions are: *How will we achieve this goal? What is the best way to achieve this goal?*

STEP 8: KEY OBJECTIVES

Key objectives, or targets, are developed for each goal. They will be SMART—Specific, Measurable, Attainable, describe a Result (not an activity), and have a Time-frame. They will be set for one year or less. They will be part of the strategic plan and also form the basis of the one-year business plan. Performance measures will be developed for each objective.

STEP 9: ACTION PLANS

Action plans will be developed for each objective. These will include short-term time-frames and indicate who will carry out the actions.

STEP 10: BUDGETS

Budgets are developed to meet the key objectives and action plans, and the overall budget is checked against the resources of the organization. If the organization cannot raise the financial resources, the strategies and priorities are revised.

STEP 11: TESTING FOR CONGRUENCE AND FEASIBILITY

The plan as a whole is checked and rechecked for congruence—between goals and objectives—and feasibility. The most common mistake is to try to do more than is physically possible for the people involved.

29 INDIVIDUAL ATTUNEMENT

PURPOSE:	To develop awareness around attuning to yourself.
FOR:	Individuals, pairs, groups.
ROLES:	Facilitator for a group.
MATERIALS:	None.
TIME:	40 minutes.

"Attunement" is the process of connecting—energetically aligning—with ourselves and others, including nature.

PROCESS:

STEP 1:
(10 MINUTES)
In the whole group, discuss what attunement might mean.

STEP 2:
(10 MINUTES)
Spend 10 minutes alone tuning in to yourself. It may be helpful to keep your eyes closed.

STEP 3:
(10 MINUTES)
In pairs, share what you notice about attunement:
Did it occur?
What was it like?
How did you get there?
What, if anything, took you away from it?
Could you go back to it?

STEP 4:
(10 MINUTES)
Go back to the whole group and share what you learned.

VARIATION:
After doing this process, do the whole exercise again and practice tuning in with one or two others. Then, as a final step, practice tuning in for 5 minutes with the whole group. (See also Process 22, *Being with a group*.)

30 ATTUNEMENT WITH NATURE

PURPOSE:	To develop awareness based around "tuning in" to nature.
FOR:	Individuals, pairs, groups.
ROLES:	Facilitator for a group.
MATERIALS:	Natural environment.
TIME:	40 to 50 minutes.

PROCESS:

STEP 1:   With the whole group, discuss what attunement might mean.
(10 MINUTES)

STEP 2:   Spend time on your own in a natural environment—walk,
(10 TO 20   run, sit or stand.
MINUTES)

STEP 3:   Reflect on these questions:
(5 MINUTES) Did attunement occur?
             What was it like?
             How did you get there?
             What, if anything, took you away from it?
             Could you go back to it?

STEP 4:   Share in the whole group what you noticed about attunement.
(15 MINUTES)

VARIATION:

Do the process again, tuning in with one or two others while in a natural environment. Sit, walk, run or stand without speaking. Then, as a final step, practice tuning in for 5 minutes with the whole group.

31 RITUAL

We all do ritualistic things. Sometimes they are "normal" things, such as drinking tea or coffee, or eating food together. They become ritual by bringing attention to them, by affirming their value. Starhawk, in her book, *Truth or Dare*, describes ritual as something that marks and intensifies value. At Zenergy we look for opportunities for ritual, and we thought that rather than merely list rituals to be repeated, we will offer some of our expressions of ritual.

MEETINGS:
We have creation and completion meetings at the beginning and end of the week. These start or end with a ritual connection, often a time of silence at the beginning. We may join hands. At the end of our meeting we may raise our hands above our heads and move our fingers or join hands, making a mountain shape in the center of the circle, and release our hands with a shout.

THEMES:
On Monday we create a theme that is a *koan* or theme for the week. This is written on our notice board and on our computer screen-saver, and is a constant visual reminder. We may chant it, sing it, use it in conversation, share it with friends and colleagues. Recent examples of our themes include: "We are grounded in being and ready to go," "Zenergy is a financially flourishing business community of whole beings."

EVENTS:
Birthdays, seasons, arrivals, departures, book publications are more ritual opportunities. If someone leaves one of our programs early, they say goodbye and the group ritually gives them a farewell. After they leave, the group reforms and recreates itself. This will include reaffirming their place in the group, and appreciation of each other.

MILESTONES:

We celebrated being a quarter of the way through writing this book by announcing it, stopping everyone and declaring it time for a drink together in the sun. When we moved into our second office, we lit a fire in the fireplace and had a ceremony to bless the room and everyone who would enter it.

GIFTS:

We were lent a beautiful East Indian rug with dragons woven into it. We met around it and took it to workshops. It became a rich focus for ritual. People sat around it, put things on it, related to the dragons and found it a source of connection and a link with other realms. We have also been given two pieces of original art, made by participants in our training programs, that we cherish and have hung on the focal wall in our office. While we traveled and worked in the United Kingdom, the United States and Australia in 1996, we were given three ornamental eggs—two alabaster and one crystal. These gifts are our treasures. We take them to our meetings and workshops. People often use them as talking sticks. (A talking stick is an object that is passed from person to person in a group. Whoever holds the talking stick may speak, and the others listen respectfully.)

32 SPEAKING FROM THE HEART

PURPOSE:	To develop the ability to speak from the heart.
FOR:	Pairs, groups.
ROLES:	Facilitator for a group.
MATERIALS:	None.
TIME:	35 minutes.

PROCESS:

STEP 1:
(15 MINUTES)

In threes or fours, take turns to speak for 3 minutes on a topic that you feel strongly about. Any topic of your choice is fine. Don't "try" to speak from the heart. Speak normally as you would to a friend about something you value.

Some topic ideas are:

My favorite place in the world.
Someone who inspires me.
A relationship I value.
A secret.
A future I want for my grandchildren.
Healing the planet.
Something I am committed to do.
Food, food, food.

Allow some time, say 1 minute, between each person.

STEP 2:
(10 MINUTES)

Each person in turn shares with the others in their small group what particularly engages their heart.

STEP 3:
(10 MINUTES)

Share the learning in the whole group. Complete with a sound that comes from the heart.

33 SOLUTION-STORMING

PURPOSE:	To generate solutions using brainstorming (Process 2).
FOR:	Groups.
ROLES:	Facilitator.
MATERIALS:	White board or large sheets of paper, marker pens.
TIME:	Choose a specific time, with 10 minutes probably being the minimum.

PROCESS:

This is a brainstorming exercise with all possible solutions being generated as quickly as possible and written down for closer scrutiny and analysis later. Remind people not to evaluate or comment on others' ideas during the "solution-storming" phase.

34 Uncovering sabotage patterns

PURPOSE:	To identify and share the ways in which each person's patterned behavior is likely to get in the way of a partnership or keep a group from achieving its purpose.
FOR:	Pairs or groups.
ROLES:	Facilitator for a group.
MATERIALS:	None.
TIME:	30 to 60 minutes.

BACKGROUND:

This is a consciousness-raising process, not an opportunity for self-blame. Keep the mood lightly serious. This is also a bold process for people who are more interested in achieving their goals than in staying safe.

PROCESS:

STEP 1:
(6 MINUTES)

In pairs, choose an A and a B. For 3 minutes, person A asks person B: *"How do you sabotage yourself?"*

Person A encourages person B to be specific and invites him or her to think of other ways: *"Yes, and how else do you sabotage yourself?"*

Examples:

"I don't speak up when I have something to contribute."
"I keep talking after someone becomes restless."
"I put myself down when I am speaking."

Swap roles.

STEP 2:
(6 MINUTES)

For 3 minutes, A asks B: *"How do you sabotage others?"* A encourages B to be specific and think of more than one way. Swap roles.

STEP 3:
(3 MINUTES PER PERSON)

In the whole group, ask everyone to share as an unstructured round. We suggest the facilitator help the group get started by sharing his or her own ways of sabotage. Remind the group that we all have our ways of sabotaging. People who don't know their patterns may want to ask the group for suggestions.

STEP 4:
(10 MINUTES)

In pairs, design an alarm system for each person's sabotage pattern (5 minutes each). For example:

For someone who interrupts others:

"If I interrupt anybody before they finish, wave at me until I stop."

For someone who lowers their voice when they are uncertain:

"If I speak too quietly, ask me to speak up."

For someone who doesn't listen to constructive criticism:

"If you think I'm not listening, remind me that I find it hard to listen to criticism, and the criticism doesn't mean you don't respect me."

For someone who finds it hard to speak about their shadow side: *"If I become quiet, ask me what it is I don't want to say."*

STEP 5:
(15 MINUTES)

Everyone shares their alarm system in the whole group, or asks for suggestions from the group if they haven't thought of one.

STEP 6:
(1 MINUTE)

Debrief from this process.

35 IDENTITY CHECK

PURPOSE:	To uncover projections made onto others.
FOR:	Pairs, groups.
ROLES:	Facilitator or timekeeper.
MATERIALS:	White board with questions on it.
TIME:	10 to 20 minutes for each person.

BACKGROUND:

We first came across this process when we trained as co-counselors. It is a useful way of recognizing projections that we make onto everyone we meet. We recommend it at the beginning of any partnership, close relationship, and when a relationship seems difficult.

PROCESS:

Participants sit facing each other, on the same level. Person A asks person B the following questions, encouraging B to answer as fully as possible:

"Whom do I remind you of?"

"How am I like that person?"

"What do you want to say to (say the name of the person)? Say it to me now as if I were that person."

"Is there anything else that you want to say to (person's name)? Say that now."

"What do you want (person's name) to say to you?"

(Person A repeats what person B says as if they were that person.)

"How am I different from (person's name)?"

"How else am I different from (person's name)?"

Person A continues to ask this question until satisfied he or she is no longer being identified with the person projected onto them: *"What is my name?"*

Swap roles.

Note: If you have positional or assigned power over the person you are having difficulty with—for example, if you are their manager or facilitator—do this exercise with someone else as a substitute.

VARIATION:
Do this process in front of a mirror, asking yourself the questions.

36 CONFLICT RESOLUTION USING ROUNDS

PURPOSE:	To provide a clear framework and safe environment to work through conflict.
FOR:	Groups.
ROLES:	Facilitator.
MATERIALS:	White board or large sheets of paper, marker pens.
TIME:	Most conflict-resolution processes take time. Allow between 1 and 2 hours depending on the size of the group. A minimum of three rounds would be 6 minutes per person, plus 15 minutes.

PROCESS:

Structured rounds (Process 1) are particularly effective for working through conflict because they provide a clear framework and a safe place for expressing strong feelings.

During this process the group expresses its hurt or upset, clarifies the issues and finds a solution—the group works through the conflict. The job of the facilitator is to empower the group by providing a structure for the group process.

STEP 1:   Encourage people to express their feelings and clarify the issue in the first round. Write down the issues as they are clarified.

STEP 2:   Have a second and possibly third round to suggest solutions. Discourage people from suggesting solutions before feelings have been expressed and really heard—this is often all that is needed. Quick-fix solutions can have the effect of ignoring feelings, and people who are upset will remain upset even though agreeing to the solution.

Encourage people to develop their thinking with each round, build on each other's thoughts and not get stuck in a fixed position. Contributions by people who have not become emotionally involved is important because they tend to see the conflict more objectively. *Remember, the facilitator does not need to have a solution—in fact, it is better not to.* Trust the group to work through the issues.

Write down the suggested solutions as they are clarified.

STEP 3:   When different solutions have been listed, have a round in which people state their preferences.

VARIATION:
Unstructured rounds (See Process 1) can be used in a similar way.

37 PROPOSING AND COUNTER-PROPOSING

PURPOSE:	To provide a structure for resolving conflict that concentrates on what can be done rather than on what can't be done.
FOR:	Groups.
ROLES:	Facilitator.
MATERIALS:	None.
TIME:	30 minutes.

PROCESS:

STEP 1: During rounds or discussion ask the key players in the conflict and others in the group to keep proposing and counter-proposing solutions—building on or sparking off one another. Encourage people to be creative and to step outside their normal thinking patterns. Encourage the group, especially the key players, to continue proposing solutions and not to get stuck in a particular position. When a solution comes up that people generally like the sound of, it will have a "ring" to it.

STEP 2: Note the proposal for fine-tuning later.

38 LISTENING FOR AGREEMENT

PURPOSE:	To use the power of listening to "hear" agreement.
FOR:	Groups.
ROLES:	Facilitator.
MATERIALS:	None.
TIME:	Variable.

PROCESS:

STEP 1: During rounds or a free-flowing discussion, the facilitator listens for agreement and encourages group members to do the same. As rounds continue, agreement may begin to emerge. Listen for this. Moments will come when agreement happens—when everyone unconsciously agrees on a solution. Someone will express a personal view, which will also be the group agreement, as yet unspoken. This is the moment to listen for. Everyone will relax slightly—*"Aha. Yes, that's it!"* Agreement has occurred. It can be "heard" by a facilitator who is listening carefully. Often it is like a bell being rung. This is the time for the facilitator or group member to intervene. These moments are important—if not captured when they occur, the group may move past agreement and go off on a tangent. Say right away: *"I think we have agreement. Let's check it out."*

STEP 2: Say what you hear as agreement and ask the group for confirmation. If the group does not confirm the agreement, continue the round or discussion. Sometimes a partial agreement can be captured. *"I think we all agree on X. Can we confirm this? Now let's continue with a round on Y."* Using this technique, it is possible to establish a number of partial agreements that together lead to a group decision.

39 FISHING FOR AGREEMENT

PURPOSE:	To provide a process for resolving conflict where participants seem to be stuck in rigid positions.
FOR:	Groups.
ROLES:	Facilitator.
MATERIALS:	None.
TIME:	30 minutes.

PROCESS:

STEP 1: Have the participants who are key to the conflict sit facing each other in a small circle, with the others seated in a larger circle around them. This is called *creating a fishbowl.*

STEP 2: Have someone restate the purpose and values of the group, the results promised and the time constraints. This will help ground the exercise in reality.

STEP 3: Encourage the key players to speak directly to each other. Have each speak one at a time in such a way as to engage the others in their own perspective. Make a time limit of perhaps 5 minutes each. Allow another 2 minutes per person for questions of clarification—not debate—from other key players.

STEP 4: Ask the key players to swap chairs (or move down, one chair to the right, if there are more than two viewpoints) and speak from the perspective of the person who was sitting there previously. Encourage them to get into role and argue passionately for the other's view.

STEP 5: Ask the key players if anything has shifted.
"What have you seen?"
"Has your view changed and can you suggest a solution?"
Continue this process until each of the key players has spoken from every viewpoint.

STEP 6: If there is still no solution, ask the outer circle to make suggestions and proposals.

STEP 7: If no solution emerges, ask the key players to meet as a subgroup after the meeting and come up with a proposal for the whole group to consider at its next meeting.

40 BOTTOM-LINING

PURPOSE:	To provide a structure for resolving conflict that acknowledges and honors people's limits.
FOR:	Groups.
ROLES:	Facilitator.
MATERIALS:	None.
TIME:	30 minutes.

PROCESS:

STEP 1: After a round, discussion or fishbowl (see Process 39), when a solution has not yet been reached, ask each key player to nominate an unaligned partner from the group, preferably someone with facilitation skills. Have this person meet the partner to explore the key player's bottom line; that is, find out what is not negotiable in the issue as distinct from a preference or want that is not essential.

STEP 2: Have the unaligned partners meet and develop a solution that takes into account and honors the bottom lines.

STEP 3: The partners then check the solution with the key players. Then ask the key players:

"Can you accept this solution?"
"Can you agree with it although you are not getting everything you want?"

STEP 4: Whether or not a solution has been found, bring the findings back to the whole group. The facilitator may want to ask the question:

"What is the cost of reaching or not reaching agreement to the project and the group?"

41 CREATING A SACRED SPACE

PURPOSE:	To encourage a sense of the sacred.
FOR:	Pairs or groups.
ROLES:	Facilitator for group (optional).
MATERIALS:	A carpet, cloth, table or area to put things on.
TIME:	3 minutes per person.

BEFORE THE PROCESS:
Invite each person to bring an item of personal value to the group. Let people know that they will be talking about it to everyone.

PROCESS:

STEP 1: Sitting in a circle, people take turns telling the story behind their item. They put it in the chosen place—on the carpet, cloth or table.

STEP 2: Allow silence at the end of this process.

STEP 3: The objects could be left in the sacred place for the whole of the meeting, seminar, workshop, or in the workplace, as participants wish.

VARIATION:
Ask participants beforehand to bring a small object they are prepared to give away that says something about some aspect of the workshop. Do the exercise as above. At the end of the workshop, have each participant identify a different object they would like to take home. This can be done either in the group or informally.

42 Finding the Higher Purpose

PURPOSE:	To find out the higher purpose of a group using a non-rational process.
FOR:	Groups.
ROLES:	Facilitator.
MATERIALS:	A container, such as a bowl or hat.
TIME:	40 minutes.

BACKGROUND:

Talk about how the "holonomic principle" asserts that the whole is represented by the part. Just as one small part of a holographic image contains the entire hologram, or just as every cell contains the DNA structure of the whole, so one person in a group can speak for the whole group.

PROCESS:

STEP 1:
(5 MINUTES)

Encourage the group to explore the possibility of using non-rational processes as a valid alternative to solve the task at hand. Would they like to try one to identify the higher purpose of the group? If so, encourage people to try it out as if it will really work. Request that they acknowledge any skepticism and be willing to experiment. Introduce the process as a ritual to discover the person who will speak for the group. In this process the spokesperson's role will be to express the higher purpose of the group.

STEP 2:
(3 TO 5 MINUTES)

Invite everyone to relax and center themselves. Suggest they focus on their breathing, breathe into their bellies and relax further on each exhale.

STEP 3: *(5 MINUTES)*	When everyone is relaxed, invite each person to put a small identifiable article, such as a watch, ring or earring, into a container.
STEP 4: *(10 MINUTES)*	Without looking into the container, the facilitator takes one object from it and gives it to the owner with the container. That person takes another object and hands it with the container to its owner, and so on. The last person to receive their object and the container is the holonomic focus and becomes the group spokesperson.
STEP 5: *(5 MINUTES)*	Taking whatever time is needed and in his or her own way, the person who is the holonomic focus—the spokesperson— centers him- or herself. The facilitator reminds the spokesperson that he or she has been ritually chosen by an agreed non-rational method. Everyone brings their energy and attention to the person. Then the spokesperson is asked by the facilitator: *"What is the higher purpose of this group?"*
STEP 6: *(5 MINUTES)*	Taking as much time as needed, the spokesperson speaks. You may want to write down the spokesperson's words.
STEP 7: *(3 MINUTES)*	After speaking, the person is thanked, he or she comes out of the role and the ritual is completed. It is important to ensure that the spokesperson is brought out of this role.

VARIATION:

The spokesperson is asked questions from the group and answers them as the holonomic focus. This variation needs to be facilitated with sensitivity.

43 EXPLORING THE SHADOW SIDE

PURPOSE:	To explore our shadow sides in a light way.
FOR:	Groups.
ROLES:	Facilitator.
MATERIALS:	Paper plates, crayons or pens, scissors, elastic.
TIME:	55 minutes.

PROCESS:

STEP 1:
(10 MINUTES)

Discuss the shadow side, or read chapter 8, *The shadow side.*

STEP 2:
(10 MINUTES)

Give everyone a few moments to think of and name an aspect of their shadow self. Share this in pairs.

STEP 3:
(5 MINUTES)

Have participants draw a mask of their shadow on a paper plate.

STEP 4:
(10 MINUTES)

Invite participants to attach elastic to their mask, to put it on, and to interact with the group, introducing their shadows to each other.

STEP 5:
(10 MINUTES)

Encourage the swapping of masks and playing each other's roles: *"Let's have fun!"*

STEP 6:
(10 MINUTES)

As a group, ask participants to remove their masks and celebrate their authentic selves, warts and all.

44 EXPRESSING THE SHADOW SIDE

PURPOSE:	To uncover and express more of our whole selves.
FOR:	Groups.
ROLES:	Facilitator.
MATERIALS:	None.
TIME:	15 minutes, plus 2 minutes per person.

PROCESS:

Talk about the shadow side or read chapter 8, *The shadow side*. You may want to share an aspect of your own shadow. Create a climate of safety.

STEP 1: In pairs, take a couple of minutes for everyone to think of an aspect of themselves that they hide, feel ashamed of or don't express to other people. Assure one another that these hidden parts are OK. Choose one aspect to reveal to the whole group.

STEP 2: Come back to the whole group. Stand in a circle. Everyone allows themselves to be aware of their shadow and names it. Each person introduces their shadow to the group by acting it out with as much freedom as they can. Do this as an unstructured round.

"I'm blaming, critical Anne, and I think people around me are stupid."

"I'm know-it-all Dale, and I want all of you to think that I'm much better than you."

"I'm moody, fed-up Bill, and I want you all to change and be fun to be around."

STEP 3: Acknowledge one another for the courage it takes to express these aspects. Sit down and share how it felt to do this exercise.

45 EXPLORING THE GROUP'S SHADOW

PURPOSE:	To give expression to the shadow side of the group.
FOR:	Groups.
ROLES:	Facilitator.
MATERIALS:	None.
TIME:	25 minutes.

PROCESS:

STEP 1:
(5 MINUTES)
Have the group divide into smaller groups of three or four to discuss the possible shadow sides of their group. In these groups, members may like to consider such issues as: where and when the group loses energy, how the group is special, what the group avoids. Is everyone in the group very nice? Does the group sabotage itself?

STEP 2:
(5 MINUTES)
Have each subgroup choose a shadow side and work out a scenario that shows the shadow side in action.

STEP 3:
(15 MINUTES)
Have each subgroup present their scenario to the whole group. The people watching name the shadow that is being acted out.

VARIATION:

An alternative process for exploring the group's shadow is to stay in the whole group and use the strategic-dialog method. (See chapter 15, *Peer inquiry.*)

PROCESSES FOR TEAMWORK

46 FEEDBACK GUIDELINES

PURPOSE:	To create guidelines for giving and receiving feedback.
FOR:	Groups.
ROLES:	Facilitator.
MATERIALS:	White board, large sheets of paper, marker pens.
TIME:	40 minutes.

PROCESS:

STEP 1:
(10 MINUTES)

In pairs, address these questions:

"What will make me more willing to give direct feedback to anyone on this team?"

"What will make me more willing to listen to feedback from anyone on this team?"

The pairs agree on their top-five key points for each question.

STEP 2:
(10 MINUTES)

Ask the pairs to find another pair, to share their key points, and then choose the top five for each question. Record these on a large sheet of paper.

STEP 3:
(15 MINUTES)

In the whole group, have participants share their key points, identify overlap and themes, and prioritize these to five points for each question. Write these on the white board. Arrange for everyone to have a copy.

STEP 4:
(5 MINUTES)

Ask the group to invent a ritual to claim their guidelines as their own.

47 CHALLENGING WITHIN A TEAM

PURPOSE:	To practice skills for challenging within a team.
FOR:	Teams.
ROLES:	Facilitator.
MATERIALS:	White board or large sheets of paper, marker pens.
TIME:	30 minutes.

PROCESS:

STEP 1:   Discuss the value of being able to challenge the group if they are not honoring their agreed culture. Suggest that the team practice doing this, and give each other feedback.

STEP 2:   Identify possible challenges that could be made in the group. Examples:

"Let's get back to the topic."
"I request that we start on time."
"I'd like to hear from some people who haven't spoken yet."
"Several people have complained about other people to me recently. I thought we agreed to take complaints directly to the people they belong to."

Invite a volunteer to practice saying one of the examples or their own version in the whole group. Team members listen for the clarity of the challenge, then give the person two-word feedback:

"Too soft." "Too hard." "Just right."

Encourage the person to use his or her own words and repeat the challenge until it is just right. If this is difficult to do, it might help to continue with other members and come back to the person, who may benefit from seeing other people meet the same challenge. Giving people another chance at it will give them a sense of success.

STEP 3:   Have participants move into pairs or threes and take turns practicing challenging the team. Encourage everyone to give feedback on the verbal and non-verbal messages, as before.

STEP 4:   In the whole group, invite people to try out their challenge, again encouraging others to give feedback.

STEP 5:   Ask if anybody has a challenge they would like to give to the group right now. Give plenty of acknowledgment for genuine constructive criticism.

48 DAY-TO-DAY FEEDBACK

Note: If you are upset about an issue, use Process 23, *Sharing withholds.* If you are clear with the person, use this process.

PURPOSE:	To share feedback with one other person.
FOR:	Pairs.
MATERIALS:	None.
TIME:	5 to 15 minutes.

PROCESS:

STEP 1: **"Will you?"**

Request agreement to give feedback to the other person.
"I'd like to give you some feedback about our project meeting. Can I do that now?"

STEP 2: **"When you."**

Give the feedback, including the specific incident:
"At the project meeting you facilitated, you didn't give anyone time to say anything at the end, and I wanted to say something."

STEP 3: **"I felt."**

Say how you felt about it:
"I felt annoyed at the end of the meeting."

STEP 4: **"I request."**

Then make your specific request:
"Please make sure we have 10 minutes at the end of our meetings to say anything we need to say."

STEP 5: **"Thank you."**

The person receives the feedback and says "Thank you." Acknowledge each other for giving and receiving direct communication.

Note: If the person who receives the withhold feels "triggered," dumped on or alienated, he or she requests a clearing session. (See Process 26, *Clearing process.*) When you use this direct communication at first, it is likely that you will feel triggered often and need a clearing session.

> **This is a vital process, so we recommend you "anchor" each step in the fingers of one hand—then you will never forget them.**

49 HOT TEAM

PURPOSE:	To develop a "hot" team—one that is especially effective and cohesive.
FOR:	Teams.
ROLES:	Facilitator.
MATERIALS:	White board or large sheets of paper, marker pens.
TIME:	1 hour, 10 minutes.

PROCESS:

STEP 1:
(30 MINUTES)
Choose an activity the team does not normally do—such as cooking a meal or a treasure hunt—for the team or subgroups of the team. You may want to include some roving observers. Have participants carry out the activity within the time limit.

STEP 2:
(5 MINUTES)
Bring the team back together, if they had spread out, and invite people to reflect on what worked and didn't work in terms of teamwork. Ask the observers to say what they noticed.

STEP 3:
(5 MINUTES)
Conduct a brainstorm on the criteria for a hot team, given the team's purpose.

STEP 4:
(5 MINUTES)
Have the group prioritize and agree on a five- or six-point criteria for their team to be hot.

STEP 5:
(15 MINUTES)
Have the team assess themselves on their performance as a team, attending to each of the criteria. They may want to use a scale from 1 to 10. Have the team keep these criteria and come back to them at regular intervals; for example, monthly.

STEP 6:
(10 MINUTES)
Using their assessments, have the team consider what it can put in place to become even hotter. Encourage team members to design an action plan that includes *who, when* and *how.*

STEP 7:
(1 MINUTE)
Encourage the team to celebrate.

50 CONSENSUS DECISION-MAKING

PURPOSE:	To practice skills of consensus decision-making.
FOR:	Groups.
ROLES:	Facilitator.
MATERIALS:	None.
TIME:	40 minutes.

PROCESS:

STEP 1:
(5 *MINUTES*)
The group chooses the form of consensus decision-making it will use. You may want to refer to chapter 9, *Team.*

STEP 2:
(2 *MINUTES*)
The group chooses a facilitator.

STEP 3:
(20 *MINUTES*)
Plan a social outing or event in which all members of the group will participate. No one may be left out.

Note: Remember to reach minor decisions along the way. Record these. Continue until one suggestion meets general approval, then work with that one. Ask those who object to propose a solution that will work for everyone.

STEP 4:
(10 *MINUTES*)
Ask what worked and what didn't work in reaching consensus. Record what you learned.

51 Resolving breakdowns

PURPOSE:	To maintain alignment and synergy in a team.
FOR:	Teams.
ROLES:	Facilitator, recorders.
MATERIALS:	White board, large sheets of paper, marker pens.
TIME:	30 minutes or so—keep up the pace without stinting on time.

PROCESS:

STEP 1: DECLARE A BREAKDOWN

A breakdown occurs when something the team is at work on isn't happening. It is not a symptom that is readily identified ("We've lost the files"); rather, it is the failure to achieve a team aspiration—that is, smooth systems. The breakdown needs to be major and worthy of serious attention by the whole team. The team aligns on the breakdown or suggests a more powerful one until alignment occurs. For example, there may be a breakdown in one of the distinctions of team. (See chapter 9, *Team.*)

STEP 2: SHARE ANY WITHHOLDS (OPTIONAL)

When a breakdown occurs, you will often find that team members are withholding in some way. Encourage everyone to express their withholds. (See Process 23, *Sharing withholds.*)

STEP 3: FIND THE COMMITMENT BEHIND THE BREAKDOWN

Clarify the team commitment behind the breakdown and state that. It may be the same as the breakdown.

STEP 4: CONVERSATION FOR POSSIBILITY

Have the team brainstorm to generate everything they can think of to resolve the breakdown. Use two scribes to write down all responses.

STEP 5: CONVERSATION FOR OPPORTUNITY

Have the team choose one or two possibilities that "speak" to them. These possibilities may "jump out" at the team from the white board.

STEP 6: CONVERSATION FOR ACTION

Ask the team to create an action plan to realize these opportunities. List the actions, when they will occur and who will take them.

STEP 7: CONVERSATION FOR MANAGEMENT

Have the team consider what management is needed for the action plan to take place—a coach, a mentor, a manager, a trainer, a buddy?

STEP 8: CELEBRATION

Celebrate the team's resolution with an energy release, such as a "whoop" or a "yo." (See Process 17.)

52 SETTING UP A COACHING OR MENTORING CONTRACT

PURPOSE:	To set up a coaching contract. You can do this at your first session.
FOR:	Person who is to be coached ("coach-ee") and coach. It can also be used for other contracts, such as mentoring or buddying.
ROLES:	As above.
MATERIALS:	Paper, pens.
TIME :	30 minutes.

PROCESS:

Consider the following questions:

What is the purpose of the arrangement?
What do you want to achieve?
How will you know when it is achieved?

Be specific here—create measurable outcomes.

What time-frame do you want for this partnership?
When will you review the contract, and how will you do this?
How will you work together?

You may want to consider issues such as:

Confidentiality. If so what will this cover? Content? Processes? Events? Personal disclosure? Everything?

Time. Is punctuality important? Having an agreed start and finish time that is kept? How long will the sessions be? Will you set up regular meetings or have phone contact? When will that be?

Availability. How accessible will you be to each other? Are there limits? Be specific—for example, "Not after 9 p.m.," "Not before 8 a.m.," "Not on weekends," and so on.

Interaction. How will you work together? Are there any patterns that you can help interrupt by naming them in your contract? For example, *say what you are thinking, don't hold back, be honest rather than nice, acknowledge feelings.*

Fees. Is there a fee involved in this arrangement? Or a barter? Any kind of reciprocal arrangement?

Record your agreement. You should both have a copy of this to refer to when you review your partnership.

(See the sample contract in chapter 10, *Coaching,* page 91.)

53 COACHING—SKILLS AND INSIGHTS

PURPOSE:	To develop skills and insights in coaching.
FOR:	Three or more people.
ROLES:	Facilitator or timekeeper.
MATERIALS:	Large and small sheets of paper, pens, markers. For each group of three: a blindfold, a ball, a container for the ball.
TIME:	1 hour, 10 minutes.

PROCESS:

STEP 1:
(10 MINUTES)
Have participants work in threes, taking 3 minutes each to recall an experience of being coached. Ask them to pay attention to what worked and what didn't work. One person takes notes or draws.

STEP 2:
(10 MINUTES)
Still in threes, participants choose roles—coach, observer and "coach-ee." The coach-ee puts on the blindfold and holds the ball. The container is placed on the ground 3 to 6 feet in front of the coach-ee. The coach coaches the blindfolded coach-ee in throwing the ball into the container for 3 minutes. Swap roles so each of the three has a turn at each role.

STEP 3:
(15 MINUTES)
Participants share what worked and what didn't, identify the learning from Steps 1 and 2, then draw or write what they have discovered about coaching on a large sheet of paper.

STEP 4:
(10 MINUTES)
Subgroups share their findings with the whole group.

STEP 5:
(10 MINUTES)
Ask participants to return to their three-person subgroup; choose a coach, a coach-ee and an observer; and practice coaching something the coach-ee wants to achieve. The observer may coach the coach.

STEP 6:
(15 MINUTES)
Subgroups share what happened with the whole group.

54 PARENTAL MESSAGES

PURPOSE:	To identify messages we received as children and their influence on our emotional development.
FOR:	Pairs or groups.
ROLES:	Facilitator, recorder(s).
MATERIALS:	White board or large sheet of paper, marker pens.
TIME:	40 minutes.

PROCESS:

STEP 1:
(10 MINUTES)
Brainstorm the parental messages that are associated with learning "how to behave," such as:

> *"Calm down."*
> *"Be a big boy for mommy (daddy)."*
> *"You'll be smiling on the other side of your face if you don't watch out."*
> *"Don't be a scaredy-cat."*
> *"Don't show your underpants."*
> Record these.

STEP 2:
(10 MINUTES)
Have the group discuss how they feel about these messages. Encourage them to express their feelings.

STEP 3:
(10 MINUTES)
Have the group make a new list of messages they would like to have received.

STEP 4:
(10 MINUTES)
Invite the group to invent, on the spot, a ritual way of claiming these new messages as their rightful inheritance.

55 EMOTIONAL CONDITIONING

PURPOSE:	To recognize sources and influences of early emotional conditioning.
FOR:	Groups of three or more.
ROLES:	Experienced facilitator.
MATERIALS:	None.
TIME:	40 minutes.

Note: Emotional outbursts may be part of this process. This needs to be recognized as healing, and not quieted or shut down completely. (For example, do not rush in with a handkerchief as soon as anyone looks as though they might cry.) Allow the person who is expressing emotions to do so, while everyone offers supportive attention.

PROCESS:

STEP 1:
(5 MINUTES PER PERSON)
Have the group divide into threes or fours. Everyone is to share an occasion they recall of being given a message as a child that stopped them expressing emotions such as rage, fear, anger, grief, excitement or exuberance. Encourage them to recall the incident in detail (place, people, surroundings, time of day, and so on) and recall the emotion of the person giving the message. If they are not sure, invite them to take a guess.

STEP: 2:
(10 MINUTES)
In the same group, have participants discuss how this incident affects them now. They should speak about their own experience.

STEP 3:
(15 MINUTES)
Have the whole group discuss their ideas on emotional conditioning in society in light of the experiences that have been shared.

56 EMOTIONAL COMPETENCE CHECK

PURPOSE:	To assess your emotional competence.
FOR:	Individuals, pairs or groups.
ROLES:	Timekeeper.
MATERIALS:	Paper, pen for each person.
TIME:	45 minutes.

PROCESS:

This process needs to be carried out in a light, accepting atmosphere.

STEP 1:
(10 MINUTES)

Read chapter 12, *Peer counseling,* and, in particular, the emotional-competence points on pages 104 to 105. These points are to be used as criteria.

STEP 2:
(10 MINUTES)

Assess yourself in relation to the criteria. Use a specific measure, such as a scale from 1 to 10.

STEP 3:
(10 MINUTES)

In pairs, take 5 minutes each to share your self-assessment.

STEP 4:
(10 MINUTES)
(OPTIONAL)

Ask for feedback from your partner for 5 minutes each.

STEP 5:
(5 MINUTES)

Discuss what you notice from doing this process.

57 THE LAUGHING MEDITATION

PURPOSE:	To free feelings and reduce tension.
FOR:	Individuals, pairs or groups.
ROLES:	Facilitator, or timekeeper for an experienced group.
MATERIALS:	None.
TIME:	15 minutes.

INTRODUCTION:
Share the purpose of the exercise and check for agreement to try it out. This exercise requires full participation, including the facilitator.

PROCESS:

STEP 1:   Everyone gets into a comfortable position in chairs or on the floor.

STEP 2:   Everyone laughs out loud for 10 minutes. If anyone is not able to laugh at any time, they hum. People are either laughing or humming at all times.

STEP 3:   Say when 10 minutes are up.

STEP 4:   At the completion of this exercise, share experiences in pairs for 3 minutes.

VARIATIONS:
• Do this exercise with your eyes closed.
• Do this exercise while able to see everyone in the group.

For other peer-development group processes, see chapter 13, *Peer-development groups.*

58 PEER-DEVELOPMENT MODEL

This model can be used as a framework and adapted to suit your peer-development group.

FOR:	3 to 6 people.
ROLES:	Facilitator or timekeeper, depending on the experience of the group.
MATERIALS:	Varies.
TIME:	2-1/2 hours, depending on number of people.

PROCESS:

STEP 1:
(5 MINUTES)
Facilitator for the session is negotiated. You may want to start with a ritual.

STEP 2:
(2 MINUTES PER PERSON)
Peers get present. (See Process 19.)

STEP 3:
(2 MINUTES)
Divide the time available equally among the number of participants, allowing 10 minutes at the end of the session to complete. One person volunteers to go first.

(CONTINUED)

STEP 4:   The first person begins by outlining what he or she wants to work on. For example: creating a project, reviewing a project, an urgent issue, a topic for which a decision is needed, a scenario for which feedback is desired.

The person then requests what he or she wants from the group. For example, constructive criticism, affirmation, suggestions, rigorous coaching, honest examples of how others in the group would handle the same situation. (See page 117.)

STEP 5:   Peers ask clarifying questions, if any, and then respond as requested.

STEP 6:   Complete the first session. The first person may want to do
(2 TO 5   any of the following, or have another idea:
MINUTES)   • Sum up what was gained.
           • Make an action plan.
           • Make a promise.
           • Request a coach for a week.
           • Acknowledge him- or herself.
           • Request applause and acclaim.

STEP 7:   Repeat Steps 4 to 6 for every other person in the group.

STEP 8:   Invite the group to say or do anything to complete the session. This may include a ritual, celebration or acknowledgment of themselves.

59 PEER-DEVELOPMENT PROCESS—INCIDENT REVIEW

PURPOSE:	To review an incident or event for which you want feedback.
FOR:	3 to 4 people.
ROLES:	Facilitator.
MATERIALS:	Pens, paper.
TIME:	25 to 30 minutes for each person, plus 20 minutes for starting and completing the group meeting.

PROCESS:

STEP 1:
(10 MINUTES)
Negotiate who will be a facilitator and who will have the first session. You may want to start with a ritual or a cup of tea or coffee.

STEP 2:
(5 MINUTES)
The first person starts by describing a particular incident in detail.

STEP 3:
(3 MINUTES)
Peers ask any questions about the incident for clarification and without discussion.

STEP 4:
(5 MINUTES)
Constructive criticism. Peers respond with any slight problems, concerns or doubts about what was described, what was revealed about the incident by the person's manner, or anything that seemed to be missing or unclear about the person's part in the incident. The person listens, sifts the feedback for what is valuable and what is not, but does not respond.

STEP 5:
(5 MINUTES)
Acknowledgment. Peers respond with full, unqualified acknowledgment, recognition and appreciation of any aspects of the person's behavior, approach, actions or attitude. The person listens but does not respond.

(CONTINUED)

STEP 6:
(5 TO 10
MINUTES)
In light of the peer feedback, the person does any or all of the following:
- Reviews their response to the situation.
- Identifies their own learning.
- Acknowledges their own handling of the situation.
- States how they would act in future.
- Says what feedback was helpful.
- Designs an action plan based on what was heard.

STEP 7:
(2 MINUTES)
The person completes this session by acknowledging themselves, celebrating, and so on.

STEP 8: Repeat Steps 2 to 7 for every other person.

STEP 9:
(10 MINUTES)
Complete the group meeting with a review of how it went for everyone. They may want to finish with a ritual.

VARIATION:

Include more people in the group and limit the number of sessions per group meeting to three or four.

60 BUSINESS-MEETING MODEL

PURPOSE:	This model provides a detailed framework for effective decision-making.
FOR:	Groups of up to 30.
ROLES:	Facilitator, timekeeper, note-taker.
MATERIALS:	White board or large sheets of paper, marker pens.
TIME:	1-1/2 hours.

PREPARATION:

Before the meeting:

- Has everyone who needs to be there been invited?
- Does everyone have the information they need?
- Are the key people attending the meeting?
- Is the room clean and welcoming?
- Are the correct number of chairs available for the people attending, and are they arranged so that everyone can see each other?
- Are all needed resources available and functioning properly?
- Allocate the following roles:
  - A facilitator to be responsible for the process.
  - A note-taker to write down decisions, agenda items and the people present.
  - A timekeeper to monitor time-frames and the end time of the meeting.

(CONTINUED)

PROCESS:

STEP 1: ARRIVAL

Greet each person on arrival. You may want to offer tea or coffee.

STEP 2: WELCOME AND RITUAL

Welcome everyone and introduce any new people. You may want to begin with a starting ritual, such as an attunement (see page 53), some kind of connection or acknowledgment. There may be special visitors to welcome or introduce.

STEP 3: GET PRESENT

Have a round of getting present (1 to 2 minutes per person). With a lot of people this could be done in pairs or threes. (See Process 19.)

STEP 4: CONFIRM DETAILS

The facilitator confirms:

- The purpose of the meeting and any specific outcomes required.
- The end time of the meeting.
- Any ground rules (optional). Everyone must agree. They may include such things as: no interruptions, no cell phones, the use of "I" statements, and not leaving the meeting until it is finished.

STEP 5: REVIEW

Review the decisions from the previous meeting. Check that all actions have been taken, and record what action has been taken. If any agreed-on actions have not been taken, attend to these quickly or note in today's agenda if discussion is needed.

Note: It is an even better practice to have a "decision manager" take care of this step before the meeting itself. This saves a lot of unproductive time. Only decisions that must be reviewed need to be referred to, and they can be placed directly on the agenda.

STEP 6: CREATE AGENDA

Create the agenda if you don't have a pre-set one. To create the agenda, each person proposes item(s) and how long they will need to cover them. Record these on a white board or large sheet of paper, placing the proposal's sponsor's initials alongside the item.

STEP 7: PRIORITY SETTING

If the time needed is longer than the available time, ask each person to select their top two items to give a group priority rating. Keep in mind:

- What items must be discussed today.
- What items are important but not urgent.
- What items can be left or attended to another way—that is, delegate one or two people to decide an action.

STEP 8: INFORMATION

Share any items of information that do not require discussion. If discussion begins, transfer the item to the agenda. It can be useful to put an information-sharing item regularly on the agenda with a time limit.

STEP 9: DISCUSSION AND ACTION

The facilitator asks the person who made the proposal to:

- Introduce the item with any useful background.
- Say what input they want from the group; for example, feedback, a decision, ideas.

The facilitator seeks clarification if needed and suggests a process, such as a round, a brainstorm or a discussion. The process is agreed to and followed. Ideas can be recorded on large sheets of paper or a white board.

If group agreement is needed, request proposals from the group until one finds general agreement. It may be helpful to reach and record minor agreements on the way. Make sure that the people making the decision are the people affected by the decision. Ask any who object what they propose instead to solve the difficulty.

When this process is complete, the facilitator summarizes, checks for agreement, and the result is recorded for everyone to see.

The timekeeper lets the group know how the time is going: *"We have 5 minutes left for this item." "Our time is up."* Assume that a decision can be reached in the time allowed. It is better not to extend the time. You may choose to come back to an item if there is time at the end of the meeting.

(CONTINUED)

STEP 10: FURTHER MEETINGS

Decide time, date, venue, purpose of any further meeting. Choose a facilitator, note-taker and timekeeper for that meeting.

STEP 11: COMPLETION

Have a round where people say anything they need to say so they do not take away any "baggage" with them. This could include anything left incomplete from the meeting, feedback to other group members, or anything they may say after the meeting. Encourage people to say those kinds of things now.

STEP 12: ENDING

You may have a ritual for ending your meeting, a summary, a connection, a song, a celebratory movement. You may wish to design your own.

RECORD-KEEPING:

Records need to include:
- People present
- People absent
- Date/Venue
- Agenda items
- Decisions made

Write down each decision as it is made. Read it back to the group if it is complex. Include specific actions, who will do them, and when they will be completed.

FOLLOW-UP:

Circulate decisions after the meeting. Or, you may choose to keep a "decision book" in a central place where everyone can refer to it. It is useful for people to work with a buddy and coach each other before the next meeting to keep the agreements they have made. Another method is to choose a decision-manager who contacts people to support them in carrying out their agreed-upon actions.

61 Zenergy business-meeting model

PURPOSE:	To provide a short framework for business meetings.
FOR:	Meetings of 2 to 10 people.
ROLES:	Facilitator, note-taker, timekeeper (optional).
MATERIALS:	Meeting book, white board or large sheets of paper; marker pens; diaries; relevant resources; records or other information.
TIME:	1 to 1-1/2 hours.

PROCESS:

STEP 1: A starting ritual—silence, attunement.

STEP 2: Roles of facilitator, recorder are claimed.

STEP 3: A round of getting present (1 to 2 minutes each).

STEP 4: Create the agenda. People propose topics and say how long they want to have the floor.

STEP 5: Prioritize the agenda. Any items of information-sharing or quick topics are identified and attended to first.

STEP 6: Work through the agenda. Record decisions, actions, who will take them and by when. Reaching agreement on controversial topics is celebrated.

STEP 7: A round of completion.

Bibliography

Bentley, Trevor. *Facilitation, Providing Opportunities for Learning.* (London: McGraw-Hill, 1994)

Bohm, David. *The Undivided Universe: An Ontological Interpretation of Quantum Theory.* (London: Routledge, 1993).

Brown, Juanita, and Sherrin Bennett. "Mind Shift," from *Learning Organizations: Developing Cultures for Tomorrow's Workplace.* (San Francisco, Calif.: New Leaders Press, 1995)

Brown, Molly Young. *Growing Whole: Self-Realization on an Endangered Planet.* (New York: HarperCollins, 1993)

Casey, Catherine. *Work, Self and Society after Industrialism.* (London: Routledge, 1995)

De Bono, Edward. *Handbook for the Positive Revolution.* (London: Penguin, 1991)

Deeprose, Donna. *The Team Coach: Vital New Skills for Supervisors & Managers in a Team Environment.* (New York: AMACOM, 1995)

Ellis, Patricia. *Swans and Angels: A Spiritual Journey.* (County Clare, Ireland: Auburn House, 1996)

Eunson, Baden. *Negotiation Skills.* (Brisbane, Australia: John Wiley and Sons, 1994)

Fox, Matthew. *The Reinvention of Work.* (San Francisco, Calif.: Harper San Francisco, 1995)

Geering, Lloyd. *Human Destiny.* (Wellington, New Zealand: St. Andrew's Trust for the Study of Religion and Society, 1990)

—*Creating the New Ethic.* (Wellington, New Zealand: St. Andrew's Trust for the Study of Religion and Society, 1991)

Gilley, Ed D., and Nathaniel W. Boughton. *Stop Managing, Start Coaching!* (Chicago, Ill.: Irwin, 1996)

Goleman, Daniel. *Emotional Intelligence.* (New York: Bantam, 1995.)

Gozdz, Kazimierz (ed.). *Community Building: Renewing Spirit and Learning in Business.* (San Francisco, Calif.: New Leaders Press, 1995)

Hackett, Donald, and Charles L. Martin. *Facilitation Skills for Team Leaders.* (Menlo Park, Calif.: n.p., 1993.)

Handy, Charles. *The Empty Raincoat.* (London: Hutchinson, 1994)

Hendricks, Dr. William, et al (eds.). *Coaching, Mentoring and Managing.* (Franklin Lakes, NJ: Career Press, 1996)

Heron, John. *The Facilitators' Handbook.* (London: Kogan Page, 1989)

—*Feeling and Personhood: Psychology in Another Key.* (London: Sage, 1992)

—*Group Facilitation, Theories and Models for Practice.* (London: Kogan Page, 1993)

—*Co-operative Inquiry: Research into the Human Condition.* (London: Sage, 1996)

Hunter, Dale, Anne Bailey and Bill Taylor. *The Zen of Groups: A Handbook for People Meeting with a Purpose.* (Tucson, Ariz.: Fisher Books, 1995)

—*The Art of Facilitation.* (Tucson, Ariz.: Fisher Books, 1995)

Leigh, Andrew, and Michael Maynard. *Leading Your Team.* (London: Nicholas Brealey, 1995)

Lessem, Ronnie. *Business as a Learning Community.* (London: McGraw-Hill, 1993)

Mackay, Allen. *Team Up for Excellence*. (Auckland, New Zealand, and New York: Oxford University Press, 1993)

Margerison, Charles, and Dick McCann. *Team Management: Understanding How People Work Together*. (Melbourne, Australia: The Business Library, 1991)

Mazany, Dr Pete. *TeamThink: Team New Zealand*. (Auckland, New Zealand: VisionPlus Developments, 1995)

Mills, Billy. *Wokini: A Lakota Journey to Happiness and Self-Understanding*. (New York: Orion Books, 1990)

Osterberg, Rolf. *Corporate Renaissance: Business as an Adventure in Human Development*. (Mill Valley, Calif.: Nataraj, 1993)

Peavey, Fran. *Heart Politics*. (Philadelphia: New Society, 1985)

Peck, M. Scott. *The Different Drum: Community Making in Peace*. (New York: Simon & Schuster, 1987)

—*A World Waiting to be Born: Civility Rediscovered*. (New York: Bantam, 1993)

Ray, Michael, and Alan Rinzler. *The New Paradigm in Business*. (New York: Tarcher/Putnam, 1993) (Note: Authors are editors for the World Business Academy.)

Reason, Peter (ed.). *Human Inquiry in Action*. (London: Sage, 1988)

Redfield, James. *The Celestine Prophecy*. (New York: Simon & Schuster, 1994)

Reps, Paul, and Nyogen Senzaki (compilers). *Zen Flesh, Zen Bones*. (Boston and London: Shambhala, 1994)

Rifkin, J. *The End of Work?*(New York: Putnam, 1995)

Robertson, Roland. *Globalization: Social Theory and Global Culture*. (London: Sage, 1992)

Scott, Mary Hugh. *The Passion of Being Woman: A Love Story from the Past for the Twenty-first Century.* (Aspen, Colo.: MacMurray and Beck Communications, 1991)

Semler, Ricardo. *Maverick: The Success Story Behind the World's Most Unusual Workplace.* (London: Arrow, 1993)

Senge, Peter M. *The Fifth Discipline: The Art and Practice of the Learning Organization.* (Sydney, Australia: Random House, 1992)

Shaffer, Carolyn R., and Kristin Anundsen. *Creating Community Anywhere: Finding Support and Connection in a Fragmented World.* (New York: Tarcher/Perigee, 1993)

Skolimowski, Henryk. *The Participatory Mind.* (London: Penguin Arkana, 1994)

Sky, Michael. 1993. *Sexual Peace: Beyond the Dominator Virus.* (Santa Fe, NM: Bear & Company, 1993)

Smart, Barry. *Modern Conditions, Postmodern Controversies.* (London: Routledge, 1992)

Spencer, Laura J. *Winning through Participation.* (Dubuque, Iowa: Kendall/Hunt, 1989)

Starhawk. *Truth or Dare: Encounters with Power, Authority and Mystery.* (San Francisco, Calif.: Harper & Row, 1987)

Wellins, Richard S, William C. Byham and Jeanne M. Wilson. *Empowered Teams: Creating Self-Directed Work Groups that Improve Quality, Productivity, and Participation.* (San Francisco, Calif.: Jossey-Bass, 1991)

Whyte, David. *The Heart Aroused: Poetry and the Preservation of the Soul in Corporate America.* (New York: Currency-Doubleday, 1994)

CO-OPERACY NETWORK
QUESTIONNAIRE

The authors of *Co-operacy: A New Way of Being at Work* are committed to organizational transformation worldwide. They invite you to discuss the ideas and content of this book with them.

Name: ....

Address: ....

....

....

Phone numbers: ....

Fax: ....

E-mail: .... *www:* ....

Organization: .... *Area of work:* ....

Comments and feedback on this book:

....

....

....

....

....

....

Please indicate your interest in networking and receiving information on

- Our facilitation training programs ☐
- Our team of facilitators ☐
- Our team of process consultants ☐
- Developing the skills of co-operacy within organizations ☐
- Other books and resources provided by the authors, available through Fisher Books ☐

Please send to authors care of:
Fisher Books, 4239 West Ina Road, Suite 101, Tucson, Arizona 85741
E-mail: **zenergy@xtra.co.nz** *or* **www.zenergyglobal.com**

Index